THE NEW SOCIETY

THE
NEW SOCIETY

BY

EDWARD HALLETT CARR

LONDON
MACMILLAN & CO. LTD
1951

PRINTED IN GREAT BRITAIN

AUTHOR'S NOTE

T HE lectures which make up this volume were delivered in the Third Programme of the B.B.C. in May and June 1951 and were published in *The Listener* : they are reproduced here without substantial change.

CONTENTS

CONTENTS

THE HISTORICAL APPROACH

TWENTY-FIVE years or so ago, when I was very young indeed and the world was not yet so uncomfortable a place as it has since become, I remember hearing a wise old gentleman remark that, in his opinion, the French revolution was a great mistake and that everything that had happened since had only made it worse. This view struck me then as novel and shocking. It has since become almost a commonplace; and, while I shall reserve for my last lecture my attempt to enquire whether the French revolution — together with its concomitant phenomena the American revolution and the Industrial revolution, which my friend would certainly have included in the category of events that had better not have happened — was or was not the starting point of a process of decline, I shall assert here and now that it was, so far as anything ever has a starting point in history, the starting point of something, and that in order to understand the problems of the " new society " in which we live today we shall have to go back at least as far as the French, the American and the Industrial revolutions.

This assertion commits me to the historical approach to the contemporary world. Modern man is beyond all precedent " history conscious ". What philosophy was to classical Greece and Rome, what theology was to the Middle Ages, what science was to the eighteenth century, that history is to our own time. The modern world is under no temptation to return to the monolithic aloofness of Thucydides, who opened his history of the Peloponnesian war with an expression of his belief that no great things had ever happened either in war or in peace before the events which he set out to describe, and evidently saw little reason to expect that any great things were likely to happen thereafter. The stoutest rationalist today finds cold comfort in the famous argument of Lucretius, the Roman sceptic : " Consider how that past ages of eternal time before our birth were no concern of ours. This is a mirror which nature holds up to us of future time after our death."

We have lost this capacity to isolate ourselves in time ; we have become incorrigibly historical in our outlook. In the Middle Ages, it was the function of history to illustrate and justify God's ways to man. After the Renaissance, history got a new start out of the process of comparing the modern with the ancient world, which was held up as a model not since attained by a degenerate posterity : Gibbon's masterpiece was the high-water mark of this school. But it was left for the French revolution to enthrone history in her own right. Condorcet, while in prison awaiting the guillotine, rejected the consolations of religion in favour of those of history, and wrote *The Outline of a Table of Progress of the Human Spirit*, in which history was seen for the first time as a progressive advance towards a future utopia. Modern history begins when history becomes concerned with the future as well as with the past. Modern man peers eagerly back into the twilight out of which he has come, in the hope that its faint beams will illuminate the obscurity into which he is going ; conversely his aspirations and anxieties about the path which lies before him sharpen his insight into what lies behind. No consciousness of the future, no history. In that nineteenth-century conglomeration of nations and potential nations, the Habsburg Empire, it was the so-called " unhistorical peoples " who were unconcerned about their future ; once they began to have aspirations for the future they discovered or invented histories of their

2

past. Between past and future, action and interaction are constant. Past, present and future are woven together in an endless chain.

The birth of modern history was bound up with the belief that the path to knowledge is the discovery of certain laws and principles whose operation is exemplified in particular phenomena. This belief had its origin in the metaphysical rationalism of Descartes and the scientific rationalism of Newton. Its application to the processes of history began in France about 1750, when Montesquieu wrote in the preface to *L'Esprit des Lois* : " I have set forth the principles, I have seen particular cases conform to them as of their own accord, I have seen how the histories of all nations are nothing but their results ". In the nineteenth century, belief became general in a principle of progress whose laws were exemplified in the events of history ; the study of history was the key to an understanding of these laws. The laws of history were thus strictly analogous to the laws of science. After Darwin it was even thought that they were substantially the same laws : Darwin had proved that evolution proceeded through the struggle for existence, the elimination of the unfit and the survival of the fittest. It suddenly became obvious that these forces were also at work in the advance of mankind through history. Progress in history and progress in the natural world were different facets of the same process. As late as 1920 J. B. Bury, in the preface to his book *The Idea of Progress*, called progress " the animating and controlling idea of western civilization ".

Intellectual fashions change rapidly (which proves that intellectuals are also human) ; and, in the thirty years since Bury wrote these words, theories of progress in history have disappeared as completely as last year's snows. They have been replaced by theories of a natural process of decay inherent in all mature civilizations and manifested by Western civilization at the present time. In 1918 Oswald

3

Spengler published in Germany his massive work which was translated into English a few years later under the title *The Decline of the West*. In 1934 Professor Arnold Toynbee began his still unfinished *Study of History*, of which six volumes were published in the 1930's. Side by side with these, though resting on a different hypothesis, may be placed the view propounded by Professor Butterfield in his broadcast lectures on *Christianity and History* in 1949. This view also represents a reaction against the theory of progress and has pessimistic implications. Here we are at the heart of our subject — the fundamental character of the changes of the past 150 years out of which the new society of today is emerging ; and in order to clear the ground I should like to begin by joining issue on certain points with these three writers whom I have chosen as the outstanding representatives of a large and miscellaneous school.

Spengler is the easiest ; that is to say, he is always clear — perhaps clearer than any profound thinker has a right to be on so difficult a subject. Spengler believes in certain historical " organisms " called civilizations obeying laws of causation which he calls destiny and which infallibly determine their cause. Spengler's system is a powerful and consistent construction which cannot be refuted within the limit of its presuppositions. It can be rejected only by denying Spengler's initial belief in the existence of civilizations as objective entities, obeying fixed laws of development and decay. Since no important thinker, at any rate outside Germany, now accepts this belief, I need spend no more time on Spengler. But he deserves a place in the record as the first begetter of the fashionable current thesis of historical decadence.

From Spengler's heady, intoxicating, enervating brew one turns with relief to Toynbee's long, cool, sparkling drink of Spengler-and-splash. In *A Study of History* Toynbee takes over Spengler's general conclusions about the course of civilizations in general and of contemporary Western civilization in particular, but tries to reach them by less Germanic paths. He stems from the English empirical tradition, and refers to what he calls on one occasion " our trusty and well-beloved method of making an empirical survey ". This presumably means that he seeks to establish the laws of behaviour of civilizations by studying how they in fact behave ; and this would be legitimate enough if he shared Spengler's view of civilizations as objective entities or organisms. But this view he explicitly abandons. For Toynbee, so far as can be judged from what he has published up to the present, civilizations are merely the name for bundles of phenomena which the historian finds it convenient to lump together ; and a subjective definition of this kind, which would be perfectly satisfactory from my point of view, seems fatal to any attempt — such as I understand Toynbee to be making — to discover laws of behaviour of civilizations. Spengler's conclusions follow logically from unsound premises. Toynbee's premises, however sound in themselves, fail to support either his main Spenglerian edifice or the sparkling cascade of historical generalizations which come so trippingly from his pen. My difference with Toynbee is that he regards history as repetitive, whereas I think of it as continuous. For him history consists of the same things happening over and over again with minor variations in different contexts ; for me history is a procession of events about which almost the only thing that can be said with certainty is that it moves constantly on and never returns to the same place. And this difference naturally affects one's view of the lessons that history can teach.

The difference turns on fundamental conceptions of the nature of history. Toynbee's view, like Spengler's, rests on the analogy between history and science in which historical thought has been enmeshed for nearly two centuries. The analogy is false. In science the drama repeats itself over and over again because the *dramatis personae* are creatures unconscious of the past or inanimate objects. In history the drama cannot repeat itself because the *dramatis personae* at the second performance are already conscious of the prospective *dénouement* ; the essential condition of the first performance can never be reconstituted. Between the two world wars a well-known military critic, having studied the conditions of land warfare between 1914 and 1918 and decided that these conditions still held, predicted that in the next war the defensive would once more triumph over the offensive. His objective reasoning may have been perfectly correct. But he omitted one factor. The German generals were determined not to repeat the unfortunate *dénouement* of 1918 at the second performance. They were thus enabled to introduce new elements into the chain of causation and to produce in 1940 directly opposite results to those predicted. Human consciousness of the past prevented history from repeating itself. Before the middle of the nineteenth century so-called bourgeois revolutions had put the middle class into power in most countries of western Europe. One result of this was a rapid expansion of the ruling middle class, and, as a result, an equally rapid expansion of the proletariat, so that Marx was emboldened to predict a proletarian revolution as the natural corollary of the bourgeois revolution. But, once this sequence of events had penetrated human consciousness, history could not repeat itself. The German middle class was by this time so frightened of the potential *dénouement* that it refused to perform the drama of the bourgeois revolution in Germany and preferred to come to terms with Bismarck. In history the presumption is not that the same thing will happen again, but that the same thing will not happen again. All analogies between history and science, all cyclical theories of history, are tainted with the fundamental error of neglecting human consciousness of the past. You cannot look forward intelligently into the future unless you also are prepared to look back attentively into the past. But this does not mean that you will find there either laws to obey or precedents to guide you. If I am deeply concerned in these lectures with the history of the last 150 years, this is not because I expect anything that happened then to happen again (this is the kind of lesson which history does not teach), but because history deals with a line or procession of events, half of which lies in the past and half in the future, and you cannot have an intelligent appreciation of one half unless you also concern yourself with the other half.

Butterfield has reacted just as strongly as Spengler and Toynbee from the doctrine of progress in history, and with more far-reaching results. Spengler and Toynbee take the doctrine of progress in the form in which it was held at the end of the nineteenth century, metaphysically in Germany, empirically in Britain, and turn it without much effort and without much fundamental change into a doctrine of decline. Butterfield jumps over the nineteenth century and the Age of the Enlightenment and lands us right back into providential history. (It seems to me fairer to call it the providential rather than the Christian view of history ; for, just as most Christians today would not believe in the intervention of God to alter the courses of the stars, so many Christians would not believe in the intervention of God in the course of current history.) Butterfield is not unwilling, like Acton before him, to identify nineteenth-century progress with the hand of providence. But the present age appears to him rather as the age of judgment in history. " The hardest strokes of heaven in history ", he writes, " fall on those who imagine that they can control things in a sovereign manner, as though they were kings of the earth playing providence not only for themselves, but for the far future " ; and this goes not only for the Napoleons and the Hitlers but for makers of the League of Nations and such-like panacea-mongers who think to build a heaven on earth.

7

But on this I would venture two remarks. In the first place, I do not know why judgment in history, which fell so heavily on Napoleon and which has fallen so heavily on recent sinners, fell so lightly on those who committed similar sins between 1815 and 1914. Secondly, while these things cannot really be measured, I should have thought that the hardest stroke of all in recent history fell on the 6,000,000 or 8,000,000 Jews who were exterminated in the camps and in the gas-chambers ; and, if I am told that this was not a stroke of judgment, but a case of unmerited suffering, then I find this conception of strokes of heaven in history still more difficult. It seems to me that belief in the intervention of providence in historical events is as hard to reconcile with serious history as belief in intervention in the movements of the stars would be with serious astronomy. History in the modern sense came into being precisely when belief in providential intervention was discarded.

This brings me to another red herring which both Toynbee and Butterfield seem to me to have dragged across the path. Both write eloquently on the theme of human wickedness. Butterfield is particularly anxious that nobody should think too well of human nature, and has some pertinent and penetrating comments on the admixture of evil in most seemingly good human actions. It would not occur to me to deny that human beings are often very wicked. Evil as well as good is of the stuff of almost everything that men do, and especially, perhaps, of everything that they do in their capacity as political animals. But this does not help us here. Our problem is to discover why, between 1815 and 1914, men succeeded in conducting their political affairs with a reasonable show of decency and without large-scale mutual destruction, and why, since 1914, hatred, intolerance, cruelty and mutual extermination have once more become the staple of political action over a large part of the world. It seems to me contrary to anything we know or anything

8

that is plausible to suppose that individual men and women today are more wicked or specifically more cruel or more aggressive than they were a hundred years ago. If they are not, we must clearly look for some different explanation of what has happened in the last forty years. Let me use an illustration suggested by Marc Bloch's admirable but unfinished *Apologie pour l'histoire*. Scientists say that there can be no fire without oxygen in the air. When my house burns down, I shall call on Professors Toynbee and Butterfield to investigate the cause, and they will explain that the fire was due to the presence of oxygen in the air. The explanation will be cogent and correct, but will not satisfy the fire assessor. The attribution of recent calamities to human wickedness equally fails to satisfy the historian.

The views which I have so far discussed all postulate the existence of objective facts of history, broadly corresponding to the objective data of science. Even Butterfield, who knows that we all approach history with our own presuppositions, still speaks of " what can be established by concrete external evidence " and of " things which must be valid whether one is a Jesuit or a Marxist ". Such things do undoubtedly exist : the exact date and place of William the Conqueror's landing in England, the number and fire-power of the ships that fought at Trafalgar or at Jutland, the statistics of population or industry or trade for a given country at a given period. These things have the same relation to history as bricks or steel or concrete have to architecture. They are facts which need to be established, tested and verified ; the historian must not be caught out using shoddy material. But they are not in themselves " facts of history ". It is only the decision of the historian to use them, the conviction of the historian that they are significant for his purpose, which makes them into the " facts of history ". That the Jesuit and the Marxist historian should agree about certain facts is of small importance. What matters is their agreement or disagreement on the question which facts are significant, which facts are the " facts of history ". " The facts of history ", says the American writer Carl Becker, " do not exist for any historian until he creates them." His choice and arrangement of these facts, and the juxtapositions of them which indicate his view of cause and effect, must be dictated by presuppositions ; and these presuppositions, whether he is conscious of them or not, will be closely related to the conclusion which he is seeking to establish. The Christian historian of the decline and fall of the Roman Empire will select different facts, and arrange them in a different way, from the historian who seeks to establish an equation between barbarism and religion. The historian who believes in the primacy of the economic factor will isolate as significant a commercial or financial transaction which, for another historian, may be as irrelevant to history as a street accident. The notion that it is possible to determine the nature of the historical process through a study of the " facts of history " is tainted with this unavoidable vice of circularity. The facts of history come into being simultaneously with your diagnosis of the historical process and as an intrinsic part of it. They cannot precede it as independent entities.

History is therefore a process of interaction between the historian and the past of which he is writing. The facts help to mould the mind of the historian. But the mind of the historian also, and just as essentially, helps to mould the facts. History is a dialogue between past and present, not between dead past and living present, but between living present and a past which the historian makes live again by establishing its continuity with the present ; and, among recent writers on the subject, I find myself most indebted to Collingwood, who has insisted most strongly on this continuity and on this process of interaction. It is an old trouble that the word " history ", which by its derivation and in its proper use signifies the enquiry conducted by the historian, should have been transferred by popular usage to the material in which he works — the series of events themselves ; for this transferred usage encourages the fallacy that history is something that exists outside the mind of the historian and independently of it. This popular usage has also encouraged confusion of thought about the so-called " pattern " in history. Needless to say, I should reject absolutely the conception once put forward by H. A. L. Fisher (and tacitly held, I suspect, by some other modern historians) of a " patternless " history, that is to say of history as an inconsequential narration having no coherence and therefore no meaning for the present. But this does not commit me to the view of a pattern inherent in the events themselves — the view of Spengler and Toynbec ; or of a pattern woven by an inscrutable providence — the view of Butterfield. For me the pattern in history is what is put there by the historian. History is itself the pattern into which the historian weaves his material ; without pattern there can be no history. Pattern can only be the product of mind — the mind of the historian working on the events of the past.

The view that the pattern of history takes shape in the brain of the historian, and is fashioned not only by the events he is describing but also by the world in which he is living, is supported by an overwhelming weight of experience ; and, although professional historians still sometimes put forward unguarded professions of objectivity, the " conditioned " character of all historical writing has now become almost a commonplace. Creators of historical systems are not exempt from this rule. The idea of progress which inspired nineteenth-century systems and the idea of cyclical movement and decline which inspires more recent systems have been transparently derived not so much from a dispassionate analysis of the past as from the emotional impact of the current situation. Even in detail those systems reflect the particular bias of those who construct them. Hegel found the culmination of the historical process in the Prussian State, Spencer in the free trade, free competition and free contract of mid-Victorian England. Spengler owed the immense popularity of his work to the occasion which it provided for his compatriots to treat the downfall of Germany in 1918 as an integral part of the predestined " decline of the west ". The deepening pessimism about the future of Western civilization which marks successive volumes of Professor Toynbee's *Study of History* reflects the increasing solicitude of the 1930's about the weaknesses and failures of British policy. Articulate human groups share a natural human inclination to attach universal significance to their own experiences. The pattern is not inherent in the events themselves ; it is imposed upon them out of the consciousness and experience of the historian. The pattern is, however, determined not so much by the historian's view of the present as by his view of the future. Past and future are the two essential time dimensions ; the present is an infinitesimally small moving point on a continuous line consisting of past and future. It is thus the future prospect even more than the present reality which shapes the historian's view of the past. Macaulay and his nineteenth-century successors were influenced not so much by their satisfaction with what they saw around them as by their conviction that things would be even better in the future. Current theories of decline in history are prompted not so much by contemplation of our present difficulties as by the belief that things are going from bad to worse. It is the sense of direction which counts.

Moreover, this insistence on the future as the criterion of judgment on the past is perfectly logical. There is point in the story of the Chinese historian who, when asked what he thought about the French revolution, replied that no serious historian could yet be expected to have an opinion about so recent an event. Macaulay regarded the nineteenth century as a century of progress, Spengler and Toynbee as a century of decay. Even if we are content with a common-sense general view of progress and do not attempt a precise definition, we have today frankly no means of deciding which view is right. Will our posterity judge the nineteenth century as the beginning of a great new period of human achievement or as the beginning of the end of our civilization ? We do not know what to think about the nineteenth century for the simple reason that the history of the twentieth century is still in the making. The historian of A.D. 2000 will be in a better case to pronounce judgment. But need we accept even his verdict — especially as it may easily be reversed by the historian of A.D. 2500 ? In modern times the shape of Roman history has changed almost from generation to generation. Gibbon found his hero in Marcus Aurelius, a philosopher-king. The age of the French revolution, which hated tyrants and liked rhetoric, saw in Cato and Brutus the pinnacles of Roman greatness ; the later nineteenth century, which had discovered the survival of the fittest, preferred Caesar ; a more recent epoch, keenly alive to the problems of planning and large-scale organization, has discerned the merits of Augustus. The question when the decline of Roman civilization began — quite apart from the more exciting question why — is still undecided by history. Two thousand years hence the final verdict on the nineteenth century may still be as uncertain as it is today. The historian is like an observer watching a moving procession from an aeroplane ; since there is no constant or ascertainable relation between the speed, height and direction of the aircraft and the movement of the procession, changing and unfamiliar perspectives are juxtaposed in rapid succession, as in a cubist picture, none of them wholly false, none wholly true. Any static view of history purporting to be recorded from a fixed point by a stationary observer is fallacious.

Let me sum up, in the light of these reflections, what I mean by the historical approach and how I think it applicable to the problems which we have to face. History seeks to link the past with the future in a continuous line along which the historian himself is constantly moving. It is clear that we should not expect to extract from history any absolute judgments, either on the past or on the future. Such judgments it is not in its nature to give. All human judgment, like all human action, is involved in the logical dilemma of determinism and free will. The human being is indissolubly bound, in both his actions and his judgments, by a chain of causation reaching far back into the past; yet he has a qualified power to break the chain at a given point — the present — and so alter the future. In common-sense language, he can decide and judge for himself, but only up to a certain point; for the past limits and determines his decision and his judgment in innumerable ways. To admit that our judgments are wholly and irrevocably conditioned is to plead moral and intellectual bankruptcy. But to recognize the conditioned element in them is the best way to put us on our guard against too readily yielding to intellectual fashions — of which the nineteenth-century belief in progress and the twentieth-century belief in decadence are excellent examples.

It is, of course, possible that this country, or western Europe, or what we call the Western world, may be doomed to perish in the near future in some sudden cataclysm from within or from without. But to accept this possibility as inevitable would be, in a famous phrase, " the treason of the intellectuals ". Certainly history can reveal no predetermined pattern which decides that a " nation " or a " civilization ", having passed through a cycle of achievement, should at a given stage wilt and perish. Nor does history provide any warrant for assuming the existence of a single entity called " Western civilization " whose destiny will follow everywhere the same uniform course. If some groups or nations within the orbit of Western civilization today are destined to decline, others of them may still provide pioneers having the energy and capacity to carry them forward along the road of fresh achievement ; at any rate there is nothing in history to prove that they cannot. Grandiose pronouncements of the judgment of history on civilizations or nations sometimes provide evidence only of the bankruptcy of the groups from which they emanate.

This backward-looking view which makes us the helpless victims of the past is one of the gravest symptoms of our present crisis. The danger which confronts us was stated more than a hundred years ago by Alexis de Tocqueville in the preface to his *Democracy in America* :

The Christian nations of our age seem to me to present a most alarming spectacle ; the impulse which is bearing them along is so strong that it cannot be stopped, but it is not yet so rapid that it cannot be guided ; their fate is in their hands ; yet a little while and it may be so no longer. The first duty which is at this time imposed upon those who direct our affairs is to educate the democracy ; to warm its faith, if that be possible ; to purify its morals ; to direct its energies, to substitute a knowledge of business for its inexperience, and an acquaintance with its true interests for its blind propensities ; to adapt its government to time and place, and to modify it in compliance with the occurrences and the actors of the age. A new science of politics is indispensable to a new world. This, however, is what we think of least ; launched in the middle of a rapid stream, we obstinately fix our eyes on the ruins which may still be descried upon the shore we have left, while the current sweeps us along, and drives us backward towards the gulf.

These words might serve as a motto to the present series of lectures, in the course of which I shall be in a constant state of war with those whose eyes are fixed nostalgically on the ruins that lie behind rather than on the prospect of the shore towards which we are travelling ; and one insidious contemporary form of this nostalgia is the profession of a so-called " neutrality " of the intellectuals, the famous ivory tower whose peculiar characteristic is that all its windows open on to the ruins of the past. Professor Oakeshott, in his recent inaugural lecture on political education, described the world of politics as " a boundless and bottomless sea " offering " neither harbour for shelter nor floor for anchorage, neither starting-place nor appointed destination ", and the only task proposed for political man was " to keep afloat with an even keel ". To keep afloat without knowing or, apparently, caring about one's port of destination seems to represent altogether too low a view of human endeavour ; nor, except perhaps in moments of desperate and mortal crisis, is it an accurate picture of how human beings actually behave. Human efforts may sometimes be feeble, and human ambitions sometimes exaggerated. But it is unwise to decry them altogether. They are the stuff of which human achievement is made ; and at the present time we suffer from too few, rather than from too many, ambitions.

Here, however, the intellectual Christian stands on the same ground with the intellectual sceptic. " Hold to Christ," says Butterfield in the concluding sentence of his book, " and for the rest be totally uncommitted." And Oakeshott's view, if I understand it rightly, might be summarized in the same formula with the change of a single word : " Hold to tradition, and for the rest be totally uncommitted ". But intellectuals cannot and should not remain " totally uncommitted " in our current predicament. Nor do they in fact remain uncommitted. " To run down philosophy ", wrote Pascal, " is really to philosophize." To denounce ideologies in general is to set up an ideology of one's own. Professions of neutrality and non-commitment are tantamount to a rejection of that " new science of politics " which Tocqueville saw to be " indispensable to a new world "; those who make these professions bury their heads, not in the sand, but in the graveyard of dead ideologies.

If, however, we resist the temptations of determinism and of scepticism, we must be cautious about yielding too readily to the blandishments of utopia. Utopianism means a rejection of the past. It denies the validity of history, substituting for it an indulgence in wish-dreams about what might have happened if only George III had not lost the American colonies, if only the internal combustion engine or the atom bomb had not been invented, if only Kerensky had beaten the Bolsheviks in 1917 — the sort of speculation that belongs not to serious history, but to the competitions column of the weeklies. In its visions of the future, it constructs imaginary commonwealths having no lineal or causal connexion with the past, and therefore unrealizable. The sane student of history must reject these wish-dreams, these speculations, these castles in the air, even at the risk of being branded as a determinist. If somebody who believes that monarchy is the best possible form of government tells me that he proposes to start a campaign for the restoration of monarchy in the United States, I shall tell him that he is wasting his time, since the history of the last 150 years is against him. But that does not make me a determinist. The function of the historian is not to reshape or reform the past, but to accept it and to analyse what he finds significant in it, to isolate and illuminate the fundamental changes at work in the society in which we live and the perhaps age-old processes which lie behind them ; and this will entail a view (which, since it will be present even if it is unconscious, had much better be consciously recognized and deliberately avowed) of the processes by which the problems set to the present generation by these changes can be resolved.

The historian undertakes a twofold operation : to analyse the past in the light of the present and the future which is growing out of it, and to cast the beam of the past over the issues which dominate present and future. His aims and purposes will ultimately be derived from values which have their source outside history; for without these history itself must become meaningless — a mere succession of action for the sake of action, and change for the sake of change. But the translation of these values into terms of policy is historically conditioned and subject to all the imperfections of the historical process; and the application of policy to a particular historical situation is also closely involved in the understanding and acceptance of that situation. Well-meaning reformers who propound utopian solutions of political problems commonly fail to recognize how far self-interest has intruded into the formulation of their ideal in terms of policy, and how complicated are the historical issues involved in its application. A historically-minded generation is one which looks back, not indeed for solutions which cannot be found in the past, but for those critical insights which are necessary both to the understanding of its existing situation and to the realization of the values which it holds.

II

FROM COMPETITION TO PLANNED ECONOMY

EXPERIENCE shows that the structure of society at any given time and place, as well as the prevailing theories and beliefs about it, are largely governed by the way in which the material needs of the society are met. In feudal Europe, as in most settled primitive communities, the unit of economic self-sufficiency was extremely small. Division of labour there was ; but, apart from the famous traditional division between " those who fight, those who pray and those who work ", it was confined mainly to the division of labour between man and woman and to the simple specialization of rural crafts. In the then conditions of transport, trade was conceivable only in luxury articles of high value for the benefit of a few privileged persons ; where it existed, it was carried on by outsiders coming from afar, and did not enter into the life of the community as a whole. Through the centuries that followed improved techniques of production led to the growth of cities, bringing the decay of the small self-sufficient unit and a new division of labour between town and country, the development of international trade and the beginnings of international banking and finance, and then, in the so-called mercantilist age, the consolidation of large potentially self-sufficient national markets. Through the same centuries new conceptions of social relations and social obligations were growing up side by side with the old patterns and gradually driving them out — first the new and revolutionary conception of the enterprising individual who enriches himself in competition with other individuals by providing services useful to the community, and then the equally new and revolutionary conception of national loyalties replacing, on the one hand, the old loyalty to the local community and, on the other, the old loyalty to the universal church and empire.

It was only when the industrial revolution brought into operation the hitherto unsuspected and unimagined productive capacities of the machine age that cheap large-scale mechanical production and cheap mechanical transport ushered in a period of unprecedented specialization and division of labour, broke through the now constricting limits of national markets, and created for the first time in history a single world economy and single world market whose blood stream was international trade and international finance, and whose nerve-centre was the city of London. The last remnants of the old conceptions of social hierarchy were swept away. The new society was to be a society of free and equal individuals. The dictates of economic morality were henceforth summed up in obedience to the laws of the market; the individual pursuing his own economic interest was assumed to be promoting that of the whole society. Minor local and sectional loyalties were merged in the larger loyalty of the individual to his nation, of the citizen to the state. It was taken for granted that even this loyalty would soon be merged in a still larger loyalty to the whole community of mankind (which was the logical corollary of the single world market) and that the citizen of a single state or nation would be superseded by the citizen of the world.

The nineteenth-century economic society produced its own corresponding political order and political philosophy ; and for a lucid and succinct summary of them one cannot do better than turn to Macaulay, that unrivalled expositor of the current ideas of his age :

Our rulers will best promote the improvement of the nation by strictly confining themselves to their own legitimate duties, by leaving capital to find its own most lucrative course, commodities their fair price, industry and intelligence their natural reward, idleness and folly their natural punishment, by maintaining peace, by defending property, by diminishing the price of law, and by observing strict economy in every department of the state. Let the government do this : the people will assuredly do the rest.

Or as Bastiat, the French economist, put it, the two principles of personal interest and free competition, " which may be judged sceptically if they are considered in separation, together create by their mutual interaction the social harmony ". In this society of free and equal individuals harmoniously competing against one another for the common good the state had no need to intervene. It did not intervene economically — to control production or trade, prices or wages ; and still less politically — to guide and influence opinion. It held the ring to prevent foul play and to protect the rights of property against malefactors. Its functions were police functions. It was what Lassalle, the German socialist, contemptuously called the " night-watchman state ".

There is no more fascinating theme in contemporary history than to follow the stages through which the *laissez-faire* " night-watchman state " of the nineteenth century has been transformed into the " welfare state " of today — at one and the same time its logical opposite and its logical corollary. The process was, of course, gradual and had begun long before the twentieth century or the first world war. While the industrial revolution was still in its infancy, Robert Owen had issued a warning against the danger of giving it its head and pleaded for state action to curb some of its consequences :

The general diffusion of manufactures throughout a country [he wrote in 1817] generates a new character in its inhabitants ; and, as this character is formed on a principle quite unfavourable to individual or general happiness, it will produce the most lamentable and permanent evils unless its tendency be counteracted by legislative interference and direction.

The humanitarian movement which led to extensive factory legislation to protect, at first the child worker and the woman worker, and later workers in general, against extreme forms of physical exploitation, were well under way in Britain in the 1840's. In the 1880's Herbert Spencer was already fighting a losing rearguard action in defence of the night-watchman state when he listed a number of recent enactments of the British parliament which contravened sound liberal and *laissez-faire* principles : these included measures prohibiting the employment of boy chimney-sweeps, imposing compulsory vaccination, and permitting local authorities to establish free public libraries paid for out of the local rates. About the same time Bismarck was sponsoring the introduction in Germany of the first system of compulsory social insurance for the workers, and thus helping to prevent, forty years later, a German Bolshevik revolution. The first social insurance measure in Britain came in the 1890's in the form of compulsory insurance of workers against industrial accidents.

Social pressures brought about these enactments in the most advanced and densely populated industrial countries before any widespread conscious departure from the *laissez-faire* philosophy could be discerned. But they were symptoms of a profound underlying refusal to accept the continued validity of that philosophy and of the presuppositions on which it rested. The conception of a society where success was, in Macaulay's terminology, the " natural reward " of " industry and intelligence ", and failure the " natural punishment " of " idleness and folly ", was not particularly humane. But it was clear-cut, logical and coherent on one hypothesis — namely that the free and equal individuals who competed for these rewards and punishments did, in fact, start free and equal. What ultimately discredited the philosophy which Macaulay had so confidently enunciated was the realization that the competitors did not start free and equal and that, the longer the competition continued, the less scope was left for freedom and equality, so that the moral foundation on which *laissez-faire* rested was more and more hopelessly undermined. How had this happened? How could the logic of *laissez-faire* lead straight to a system which seemed its opposite and its negation?

In Great Britain and in the chief European countries, the Industrial revolution broke in on a long-standing traditional order based on social hierarchy. The economic and social inequalities left behind by the *ancien régime* made impossible anything like the clean start between the competitors which was assumed by the exponents of *laissez-faire*. But this flaw, much less in evidence in the new world of America than in old Europe, was not very important. What was far more serious was that the revolution, which purported to wipe out the old inequalities and did in large measure wipe them out, soon bred and tolerated new inequalities of its own. The notion of a society in which individuals start equal on equal terms in each generation — the unqualified recognition of *la carrière ouverte aux talents* — is soon tripped up by what seems to be a deep-seated human instinct. However firmly we may in theory believe in an equal start for everyone in the race, we have no desire that our children should start equal with the children of the Joneses — assuming that our greater wealth or more highly placed connexions enable us to give them the initial advantage of better nutrition, better medical care, better education or better opportunities of every kind. Twenty years ago a school was started in the Kremlin in Moscow for children of high party and Soviet officials. Nobody supposes that its function was to enable these children to start equal with other Russian children. And so, in every society, however egalitarian in principle, inherited advantages quickly set in motion the process of building up a ruling class, even if the new ruling class has not the additional asset of being able in part to build on the foundations of the old. And so it happened in the industrial society of the nineteenth century; and the story of the industrious errand-boy who became the managing director and of the lazy son of the managing director who became an errand-boy was soon an agreeable myth which took little or no account of the facts of life. But, when this myth was exploded, it carried away with it whatever moral justification had existed for the non-intervention of the state in a society where industry and intelligence were automatically rewarded and idleness and folly automatically punished.

Nor did the trouble stop there. What was much worse than any inequality of initial opportunity was the fact that individuals engaged in the economic process obstinately refused to remain individuals. Instead of competing against one another on equal terms for the good of all, they began to combine with one another in groups for their own exclusive profit. Mr. Paul Hoffman, when he was Marshall Aid administrator in Europe, once remarked in a broadcast that there was nothing like competition for keeping business men awake at nights. The picture of American business men tossing from side to side in sleepless beds and haunted by nightmares of competition may well be correct; according to British social mythology, British business men play golf and enjoy dreamless sleep. But Mr. Hoffman told only half the story. For three-quarters of a century American as well as other business men have been thinking night and day about competition. They long ago decided that it was an evil to be got rid of as thoroughly as possible in the branches of industry or trade in which they earned their profits; and since they were intelligent and ingenious men, they have on the whole been remarkably successful in doing so. The nightmare of competition has been replaced by the dream of monopoly. During this long period the individual business man has been ousted by the company, the company by the cartel and the trust, the trust by the super-trust. In this process the sky is the limit ; nothing short of monopoly, first national, then, in favoured cases, international, is the ultimate goal. The general pattern is hardly affected by the survival of a host of small men in out-of-the-way places or in other than key industries ; these are now no more than the hangers-on of modern economic society, directly or indirectly dependent on the big concerns, tolerated in lines of business where no large profits are to be earned and debarred by their isolation from exercising any real economic power. The continuous and progressive replacement of the smaller by the larger unit has been the typical trend of economic organization in our time.

It is an illusion, still fostered by that select group of business men of whom Keynes once said that they " are generally the slaves of some defunct economist ", that monopoly is wicked and inefficient. Every human institution has its share of abuses arising from human wickedness. But it would be hard to prove that the abuses of monopoly are more widespread or more wicked than the abuses of competition. Let me quote from a recent biography by a well-known American writer of perhaps the greatest of the American financiers and trust-builders — *The Great Pierpont Morgan*, by F. L. Allen :

By instinct, if not by reason, most business men hate competition. . . . A man's competitor is the fellow who holds down his prices, cuts away his profits, tries to seize his markets, threatens him with bankruptcy, and jeopardizes the future of his family. . . . It is hardly an accident that most of the Americans who at the beginning of the twentieth century were charged with being monopolists had got a good look in their youth at competition at its savage and unbridled worst and had decided to do something about it.

I hold no brief for the Pierpont Morgans ; but neither do I see anything particularly noble about unbridled competition, " red in tooth and claw ". Nor is the choice today between monopoly and competition, but rather between monopoly and what economists call " oligopoly " — that fig-leaf which serves to temper the shock of monopoly to a prudish public and to evade ill-conceived anti-trust laws — the system by which two or three powerful groups flourish side by side in the same field on the basis of written or unwritten price-fixing and market-pooling agreements. Oligopoly offers most of the abuses of monopoly without its efficiency. The man who thanks God he is not a monopolist may easily be something worse.

This summary outline is enough to show that contemporary forms of economic organization, while they are in one sense a direct negation of the *laissez-faire* system, in another sense proceed directly from it. The result of free competition has been to destroy competition ; competing individuals have replaced themselves by monopolistic groups as the economic units. The further, however, this process advances, the more untenable becomes the conception of non-interference by the state. The philosophy of *laissez-faire* presupposed the free competition of individual employer and individual worker on the labour market. The capitalist system in its maturity offers the picture of a class struggle between two vast power-groups ; the state must intervene to bring about that modicum of harmony which *laissez-faire* so conspicuously failed to produce, and to mitigate the harshnesses of a struggle which, carried to its extreme conclusion, would wreck the foundations of the existing order. Hence the development of factory legislation, social insurance, wage-fixing and legislation against strikes. But the philosophy of *laissez-faire* also assumed that the consumer would call the tune of the economic process, that his word would be law and his decision final. Capitalist reality shows the unorganized consumer, the typical little man of modern society, helpless before the battery of monopoly, price manipulation, salesmanship and mass advertising trained upon him by the highly organized and competent producer ; the state must intervene, by price-fixing and quality controls, to protect the consumer against the overwhelming power of organized capital, sometimes supported on this issue by organized labour. Nowhere has state intervention been more widely solicited than by the small consumer seeking protection against the allegedly inflated prices and profits of the large producer. Finally, in times of extreme scarcity, the state must intervene to ensure an equal distribution of limited supplies to meet the minimum requirements of each and all.

Historically speaking, however, it was neither the need to mitigate the struggle between capital and labour nor the need to protect the consumer which drove the last nail into the coffin of *laissez-faire* capitalism and provoked massive state intervention in every function of the economy. This was brought about by the problem of mass unemployment. The final blow was struck by the series of economic crises culminating in the great depression of the early 1930's. In orthodox capitalist theory, crisis was the catalyst which purged unsound and unhealthy elements from the system, the regulator which readjusted the delicate balance of supply and demand, the court of appeal which rewarded the industrious and the provident and condemned the foolhardy and the negligent to perdition. It was part of the normal procedure of punishing and expelling the inefficient, and operated as such in the nineteenth century with comparatively moderate results in economic dislocation and human suffering — results which were accepted as the proper and inevitable cost of a working economic system. But in the twentieth century both the practice and the theory of periodic economic crises were rejected as intolerable — partly because humanitarian people refused any longer to believe that men who had so brilliantly mastered the secrets of material production were unable to devise some less wasteful and preposterous method of organizing distribution, but mainly because the great organized forces of capital and labour now both revolted more and more sharply against each successive crisis and turned more and more impatiently to the state to rescue them from its impact. If the cry for help came even more strongly from the side of capital than from that of labour, this was probably because the capitalists had closer affiliations to the ruling class and more direct and impressive means of access to its ear. The Federation of British Industries and the National Union of Farmers were more effective forces than the trade unions in determining the course of British economic policy in the great depression ; and, when the blizzard struck the United States, it was the bankers, the farmers and the industrialists who turned most desperately and most eagerly to Washington with the plea to come over and help them.

It was thus the capitalists — the industrialists, farmers and financiers — who, unwilling to see the capitalist theory of the elimination of the unfit through periodic crises applied to themselves, begged the state to save them by laying the foundations of an ordered national economy. They were fully justified in so doing. The structure of industry and finance in the twentieth century had been so firmly integrated and concentrated that its main sectors were no longer separable either from one another or from the national economy as a whole. It was unthinkable that a great bank or a great railway, a major unit in the steel or chemical industries, should be wound up for failing to meet its obligations. Far from watching the economic struggle from heights of Olympian aloofness, the state had to step into the ring in the national interest to save the potential loser from being knocked out. No doubt, the bankers and industrialists who in the hour of distress invoked state support did not fully realize the implications of their action ; no doubt, they hoped that the state, having saved them from destruction in bad times, would allow them in good times to resume their unimpeded progress in earning profits under the flag of private enterprise. But this was to overlook realities. What had once been done could not be wholly undone : still less could it be expunged from the records or its lessons unlearned. For what had been clearly demonstrated in the moment of crisis was that the national economy was one and indivisible. The concentration and enlargement of economic units had gone so far that there was now no logical stopping point short of the nation as a whole — and perhaps not even there. The conception of a national economy had taken root ; and by the same token some kind of planning authority had become inevitable, whatever its name and purposes, however its functions were defined, and through whatever agencies or methods it operated.

The same broad developments occurred in all the leading industrial countries though with many variations and, above all, differences in tempo due to different economic conditions. They would today be accepted as almost uncontroversial but for the practice and precept of the United States. American capitalism was an exceedingly active and powerful growth which reached maturity considerably later than European capitalism, and reaped advantage from the time-lag in the form of higher mechanical efficiency. The first world war, which laid waste the economies of Europe, gave an immense stimulus to American industry. After that war the United States became beyond dispute the leading economic power, and the protagonist in an attempt to restore all over the world the shattered foundations of the capitalist order. The attempt, bolstered by a large-scale revival of international lending under the sponsorship of American banks, foundered in the great depression of the early 1930's. Though the great depression was in its origin an American crisis spreading across the Atlantic over Europe, its lessons were more fully taken to heart, and more readily accepted as conclusive, in shattered Europe than in the still relatively intact economy of the United States. In the European countries, as well as in Great Britain, it became an axiom that another capitalist crisis could never be allowed to occur and that it was a primary duty of the state to prevent it from occurring. Acceptance of this axiom marked the final rejection of the *laissez-faire* philosophy ; and, in so far as historical endings and beginnings can be precisely dated, the unplanned and uncontrolled capitalist system of the nineteenth century everywhere outside the United States was dead in 1933. In the United States the early days of the New Deal saw the same eager panic-stricken flight as elsewhere from the consequences of an unplanned capitalist order. But in the United States the unrivalled strength of the economy, un-ravaged by the first world war and its sequel, was sufficient, once the immediate danger was over, to allow of the survival and partial recovery of the *laissez-faire* tradition. Much that was done in the New Deal was never undone. The ultimate control of financial policy passed from the banks through the Federal Reserve Board to the Treasury ; sub-sidies and price-fixing remained in more than one sector of the economy ; social insurance had come to stay, though still on a modest scale by British standards ; and TVA repre-sented a significant excursion into regional, though not yet national, planning. Yet these things were forgotten in the general assumption that the old ship, having shed a little ballast, had successfully weathered the storm, and that the United States was still a stronghold of *laissez-faire* and private enterprise.

It has thus come about that after the second world war American policy was still publicly and privately committed to the defence of private enterprise and apparently oblivious of the immense inroads that had been made into it, even in the United States. A highly artificial attitude came to prevail. The defence of private enterprise became a required article of faith of an established church. Many professed, with varying degrees of sincerity, to believe in something they no longer really believed in; others sincerely believed in what they no longer practised; most of all repeated the creed without asking what it meant. The performance of these rites does not alter the fact that private *laissez-faire* capitalism, dead everywhere outside the United States for twenty years, has there too been mortally stricken. Today, in the aftermath of the second world war, the criteria of *laissez-faire* are no more accepted in the United States than in any other Western country as an adequate guide to economic policy. The principle of state intervention and control is tacitly admitted; the only difference is in the greater or less efficiency of the intervention and in the greater or less frankness with which the rôle of the state is admitted. During the first half of 1951 the major issues of American economic policy were price-fixing and wage-fixing; and controversy turned only on the question where to fix them, not whether to fix them. The principle was no longer contested.

At this point two arguments arise which are not important in themselves but are sufficiently current to call for a brief comment. The first argument rests on a simple syllogism. The United States is a country of private enterprise; the United States is the most prosperous country in the world; therefore private enterprise means prosperity. The same argument sometimes appears in a historical rather than a geographical form. The nineteenth century was the century of *laissez-faire*; it was also a century of prosperity; therefore *laissez-faire* means prosperity. The argument is one of those which holds good " other things being equal " —

which, of course, they never are — the fallacious assumption of equality being in this case made between the United States and Europe or between the economic conditions of the nineteenth and twentieth centuries. The other argument is slightly more sophisticated. It is suggested that the nineteenth century *laissez-faire* capitalist order was undermined not by the emergencies to which it was exposed between the two world wars, but by the wrong measures taken to deal with these emergencies. What was strangling capitalism, on this hypothesis, was not a process inherent in capitalism itself, but the measures of control, restriction, rationing and planning adopted by governments in defiance of the true principles of *laissez-faire*. This argument contains an element of purely abstract truth. In theory, if it had been possible everywhere in the 1920's and 1930's to apply the principle of absolute non-intervention by the state, and if capitalists themselves could have been prevented from combining to protect themselves against the free working of the capitalist system, the economic balance would in the long run have readjusted itself. But this was the " long run " in which, as somebody once said, we shall all be dead. Such readjustment would have called for an entirely new pattern of world economy, a shifting of centres of production from continent to continent, an intensification of existing inequalities between man and man and between nation and nation, and the unemployment, transplantation or final extinction of vast populations. This fantastic nightmare is a sufficient answer to the plea that there was nothing wrong with the capitalist system, but only with the measures taken by governments — or by capitalists themselves — to interfere with its free operation.

Throughout the above discussion, much has been said about capitalism and something about planning, but nothing at all about socialism. " Socialism " is a difficult word. Marx, when he first distinguished " scientific " from

" utopian " socialism, used the words " socialism " or " communism " indifferently to describe the economic order which would follow the inevitable downfall of capitalism ; to the " anarchy of production " under capitalism would succeed the " socially planned " economy of " socialism ". Later Marx himself distinguished between two stages of what he called " socialism " or " communism ". The first stage would introduce a planned economy, but would still be marked by survivals of the capitalist order, and would continue to use processes of exchange and payment both for goods and for labour ; the second stage would usher in the society of the future based on the principle " from each according to his capacities, to each according to his needs ". Later Marxists introduced a distinction unknown to Marx himself between the words " socialism " and " communism ", reserving " socialism " for the first of Marx's two stages, and " communism " for the second ; it was in this sense that Stalin announced in the 1930's that Russia had achieved a socialist society and had started on the road to communism. Since the 1920's it has been customary to reserve the word " communism " for the current Soviet régime of planning combined with the methods of the police state and " socialism " for attempts in other countries to combine planning with a maintenance of the old principles of democracy as well as with far-reaching social policies of " fair shares for all " — what is sometimes called " the social service state " or the " welfare state ". A sharp line, unknown to the nineteenth century, has been drawn between " socialism " and " communism ", corresponding to the historical split between the Social-democrats of western Europe and the Russian Bolsheviks. It is in this sense that the word socialism will be used here ; and, so far as British politics are concerned, I shall use it without party implications. It was a well-known Liberal who, sixty years ago, coined the famous aphorism : " We are all socialists now ". Today, the Conservative party programme has a marked socialist colouring.

These explanations lead up to the question of the relations between planning and socialism. Professor W. A. Lewis has recently written that " the dispute about planning cuts right across Left and Right, and has nothing to do with the dispute about socialism ". This is an over-statement of an important truth. In the middle of the last century Marx set out to prove that the capitalist system, in virtue of what he called the " contradictions " inherent in it, was doomed to self-destruction ; the " anarchy of production " under capitalism would, by this inherent process, be transformed into a socially planned economy. While some of Marx's arguments have been rebutted, some of his prophecies falsified, his main analysis of the impending decline and fall of nineteenth-century capitalism has stood the test of time and experience. But, when Marx assumed rather than sought to prove that the planned economy which would replace the defunct capitalist order would be identifiable with socialism, he made a jump which has not yet been justified by the sequel and about which controversy is still possible.

Every revolution, though it has deep underlying causes, is the immediate product of an emergency. Historically the emergency which hastened the transition from *laissez-faire* capitalism to planning was not social upheaval but war. The motive force behind the change was the demand not for social justice, but for national efficiency (except in so far as it can be said that some measure of social justice is in itself a condition of national efficiency in modern war). The occasion was the first world war, and the country which led the world along the path to planning was Germany. Nor was this an accident. Germany in 1914 was the most advanced capitalist country in the world in the sense of being the country where the national economy was most firmly welded together through a series of trusts and cartels, and above all through the great banks, into a single entity which, side by side with the army and in close alliance with it, dominated the state. The Social-democrat Hilferding, in a famous work published in Germany in 1909 under the title *Finance-Capital*, declared that it would suffice to take over six large Berlin banks in order to take control of German industry. When war broke out, the framework was already prepared ; after more than a year of fumbling and confusion Walther Rathenau, son of the founder of Germany's largest electrical combine, was called to the German War Ministry, and built with astonishing ease and celerity the main structure of the German planned war economy.

Before 1914 nobody had clearly recognized that a war economy differed fundamentally from a peace economy. Ten years earlier a British select committee had rejected a project to accumulate stocks of food and other essential commodities in Great Britain against the contingency of war on the plea that it would be more economic to import what was required when the war actually occurred. The German military plan to invade Belgium was not extended to Holland on the ground that Rotterdam must be left neutral for the passage of German overseas trade. " Business as usual " was the slogan under which the first period of the war was conducted in Great Britain. But the course of the first world war settled for all time the question of the indispensability of a planned economy for national efficiency in the war. After 1918 this view sank into the consciousness of all parties in all countries and became uncontroversial. Hitler, whose party programme had lost the socialist component even before he rose to power with the aid of the industrialists, was responsible for the next innovation. His introduction of a peace-time planned economy cured the evil of 6,000,000 German unemployed. But Hitler conceived and justified it, not as a social, and still less a socialist, programme, but as

35

a programme of rearmament. From this point onward it became an accepted doctrine everywhere that planning could be justified not only by the contingency of war itself, but by the need to prepare for war. The eagerness with which this doctrine has been accepted is illustrated by the present situation in the United States, where measures of economic planning, which would have been rigorously contested if they had been put forward as items of a social programme, win enthusiastic support as necessary contributions to national preparedness for war.

We have thus arrived at a paradoxical position. *Laissez-faire* individualist capitalism — the régime of private enterprise in the true sense of the term — has evolved by an inherent process of development into monopoly capitalism. Monopoly capitalism has provoked and made inevitable the intervention of the state as a more or less active directing force in the economic order. This is the system which in its fully developed form is known in English as " planning ", in German as " *Planwirtschaft* ", in French as " *une économie dirigée* " and by Marxists as " state monopoly capitalism ". But this system — which, whatever it is, is not socialism — is confronted by an unexpected difficulty.

The advantage of the *laissez-faire* philosophy of which capitalism in its heyday was the practical expression was that it dispensed with the need to formulate any aim of economic policy. The consoling assurance was offered to the individual that, in promoting his own economic interest, he was equally promoting that of the community. But once the practice and philosophy of *laissez-faire* were abandoned, some purpose had to be defined, or at any rate silently assumed, which would guide the intervention of the state.

Any kind of state control or state planning automatically raises a number of questions which cannot be dismissed with a vague appeal to efficiency. The questions, Efficiency for What ? and Planning for What ? become acutely practical ;

for the answers to them determine our policy. The nineteenth-century capitalist order has been transformed by a process of historical evolution into a system where state intervention and state planning are imperative. What is still uncertain and still controversial is the purpose for which the state intervenes and plans. It is a tragedy of our generation that the only purpose for which planning is yet universally admitted as necessary and legitimate is the contingency of war. This choice is obviously the simplest. Any kind of planning involves irksome controls ; nearly everyone will accept the inconvenience of controls and restrictions in order to make his nation militarily secure and militarily powerful. It is the choice which is most likely to appeal to the largest and most powerful groups in industry. Hitler made it at a time when he was under heavy obligations to the big German industrialists and could scarcely have afforded to antagonize them. It provides full employment and can therefore be made acceptable to the worker. The dilemma of this choice is, however, its transient and impermanent character. It is not my task to discuss current rearmament policy. Nothing that I have to say is intended to support the view that Britain has at the present time reached the physical or psychological limits of her capacity. But, taking a long-term view, such limits obviously exist — for Britain as for other countries. Neither a war economy nor a rearmament economy provides a conceivable basis for a lasting social order. War itself would not solve the problem — except for those whom it annihilated altogether. Whatever was left after the war would have to take up again the planning of a social and economic order directed to some other purpose, and judged by some other criterion, than that of efficiency for war.

If, therefore, my interpretation of history and my diagnosis of the present and future are sound — and in these lectures I can claim to offer no more than my own interpretation and diagnosis and to show how they are intertwined with one another — we have reached a point in history where the process of transition from the nineteenth-century *laissez-faire* capitalist order offers us no alternative, short of annihilation in war, to a social and economic order which we can call the " welfare state ", the " social service state ", or simply " socialism ". It has often been said that war is a forcing-house of socialism. The same is partly true even of re-armament, since the diversion of scarce resources to purposes of defence clearly involves a new emphasis on equal distribution of what remains — a policy of " fair shares for all ". But the essence of socialism resides in the manner in which production is organized, in the purposes which inspire the public control and planning of the economy. You cannot in these days plan for inequality. Once you can no longer explain inequalities either as the salutary result of a natural economic process or as incidentals in an economic organization primarily designed to prepare for war, it must become a main purpose of economic policy to eliminate them. This is the political connexion between planning and socialism. In theory, they are separable ; historically, they spring from different sources. But, once the historical evolution of the capitalism system has made a controlled and planned economy necessary, and once the temporary expedient of planning for war has become obsolete, to plan for socialism is the only available alternative.

This dilemma also provides the key to another disputed question — the relation between democracy and socialism. Both words are vague and susceptible of varieties of inter-pretation. But they are widely accepted as the embodiment of the political and of the economic aspirations of the modern world. It has often been said that the liberty and equality of political democracy are hollow unless they are completed by economic liberty and equality ; Babeuf lost his head for saying it first in 1797. So long as democracy remained the political partner and counterpart of *laissez-faire* capitalism, responsibility for the workings of the economic system could be rejected as beyond the reach of the political arm. But, once state intervention in the economic process is accepted as legitimate and inevitable, political responsibility for economic ills can no longer be declined. We have reached a stage when the realization of Babeuf's dream has become imperative.

It is this task of combining political and economic goals, of reconciling democracy and socialism, which, after the second world war, inspired the social policies of Great Britain and of some of the smaller European countries. The possibility of the attempt to make political liberty compatible with planning for socialism has been challenged from both sides. It is denied by the communists — not indeed, explicitly, but implicitly in the practice of Soviet Russia. It is equally denied by those old-fashioned democrats whose conception of democracy is still rooted in the derelict philosophy of *laissez-faire*. The second challenge is rendered particularly insidious by the current international emergency; for those who denounce planning as incompatible with democracy when it is directed to social ends, readily accept planning when directed to preparation for war. A body of opinion is thus unconsciously created which justifies planning for war as essential for democracy while it condemns planning for socialism as incompatible with democracy. Yet, in so far as the issue turns on the prospects of democracy, the distinction is fallacious. Experience shows that, whatever the difficulty of reconciling democratic freedoms with socialism, many of these freedoms are immediately vulnerable to war or intensive preparation for war. To reconcile democracy with planning for socialism is a difficult task. It may have been undertaken too late. But it is the only course which may yet, if war can be avoided, enable democracy to survive.

III

FROM ECONOMIC WHIP TO WELFARE STATE

THE relation of the individual to society, of the citizen to the state, is the subject matter of political philosophy and of most practical political problems. Everyone admits that the individual has some rights as against society; everyone admits that the individual has obligations to society; and everyone except the anarchists agrees that society is entitled, through its organ, the state, to enforce observance of those obligations by the individual. But where the line is drawn between the rights of the individual and those of society — or, to put it differently, what is the balance between the rights and the obligations of the individual in society — is an empirical question which men have settled in very different ways at different periods of history. In the feudal period of European history the rôle of the individual in society was determined by hereditary status combined with ownership of land, and social relations were woven round a traditional framework of mutual obligation founded on hierarchy; and so solid and resistant was the structure that centuries of gradual change were required to undermine and destroy it. It was left to the French revolution, following the trail blazed by the English revolution and joining hands with the Industrial revolution, to strike the final blow. Society founded on hierarchy — though even then only in western Europe — was at last swept away. The new society was to be in principle a society of free and equal individuals. Relations between them were henceforth to be determined not by status, but by contracts entered into by them of their own free will.

No period before the nineteenth century would have questioned the right of society to compel men to work. In many societies certain classes of the population were exempted from " work " in the narrower sense ; in some countries work in this sense was performed mainly by slaves. But that the working classes — or " the poor " as they were customarily called in England until well on into the nineteenth century — were under an obligation to work, and that this obligation, like any other social obligation, could and should if necessary be enforced by law, was taken for granted. English legislation of the Tudor period, when the sanctions of the mediaeval order were breaking down, was explicit and severe : persistent vagrancy was a capital offence. The parish had the duty of providing relief for the indigent. But this was coupled with the duty of compelling the able-bodied among them to work for the parish. So long as the feudal organization of society prevailed and the local community remained strong, the legal and moral compulsion to work had been offset by the legal and moral obligation of society to see that nobody starved in bad times. Poverty was not yet either a sin or a disgrace ; the attitude towards the relief of the indigent was comparatively tolerant. But when the foundations of capitalism were laid, and organized manufacture with hired labour became common, voices began to be raised against this leniency. In 1704 Defoe published a pamphlet entitled *Giving Alms no Charity and employing the Poor a Grievance to the Nation*. He argued that if the poor were relieved they would remain idle, or alternatively that, if they were set to work in public institutions, the private manufacturer was equally deprived of his source of labour, the conclusion — expressed in modern terms — being that they should be thrown on the labour market and allowed to starve if they failed to find a place there. A few years later Mandeville's *Fable of the Bees* pointed the conclusion that the poor " have nothing to stir

them up to be serviceable but their wants, which it is prudence to relieve, but folly to cure ", and that " to make
society happy it is necessary that great numbers should be
wretched as well as poor ".

The Industrial revolution, beginning to gather momentum in Great Britain towards the end of the eighteenth
century, completed the transformation. Its demand was
nothing less than to drive a hitherto predominantly rural
working class into urban workshops and factories. No social
habit impelled men and women towards this novel and
unattractive form of employment. To create this habit the
strongest compulsions and incentives would be called for.
The enclosures were providing the motive force to drive the
workers off the land. But the force could no longer operate
fast enough or powerfully enough if the brake were applied
in the form of relief which enabled the unemployed or underemployed to remain where they were. In 1785 William
Townsend in his *Dissertation on the Poor Laws* put the case
against the old system without squeamishness :

Hunger will tame the fiercest animals, it will teach decency
and civility, obedience and subjection, to the most perverse. In
general it is only hunger which can spur and goad them [the poor]
on to labour ; yet our laws have said they shall never hunger.
The laws, it must be confessed, have likewise said they shall be
compelled to work. But then legal constraint is attended with
much trouble, violence and noise ; creates ill will, and never can
be productive of good and acceptable service ; whereas hunger is
not only peaceable, silent, unremitting pressure, but, as the most
natural motive to industry and labour, it calls forth the most
powerful exertions ; and, when satisfied by the free bounty of
another, lays lasting and sure foundations for good will and
gratitude. The slave must be compelled to work, but the free
man should be left to his own judgment and discretion ; should
be protected in the full enjoyment of his own, be it much or
little ; and punished when he invades his neighbour's property.

42

There might have seemed something ironical about the " judgment and discretion " left to the free worker to starve at will ; but this is perhaps the first occasion in literature on which the dilemma of the choice between freedom from want and freedom from legal constraint was so cogently and uncompromisingly put.

Though William Townsend was a less original and distinguished writer than Defoe or Mandeville, the seed now fell on prepared ground and the *Dissertation* proved fruitful. Just half a century was required to complete the change-over. The Poor Law of 1834 finally abolished all grants in aid of wages, restricted outdoor charitable relief within the narrowest limits, and established the workhouse system as it was known in the nineteenth century. The laws no longer compelled anyone to work. Forced labour was henceforth a term of opprobrium. For the troublesome, violent and noisy system of legal constraint had been substituted the peaceful, silent, unremitting pressure of hunger. The worker was a free man " left to his own judgment and discretion ". He was free to starve with his family, to enter the workhouse (in which case he would be separated from his family) or to enter the factory. So long as care was taken to make life in the workhouse harsher and more degrading than the life of a factory worker, the end was achieved. The labour revolution was complete. Labour power was a commodity sold by its owner and bought by the employer who wanted it under a freely negotiated contract. The labour market, which was a necessary part of the *laissez-faire* capitalist system, had been established.

It will not be supposed that the builders of the new industrial society had consciously thought out this new labour policy ; vital decisions were taken in the piecemeal and haphazard way in which great historical changes commonly occur. Nor should we assume that those who created this system were cruel or unenlightened men. They accepted the postulate that Britain must be industrialized; and I am not clear by what standard they should be condemned for accepting it. If, however, Britain was to be industrialized, it was necessary to recruit workers and compel them to work when and where they were needed — just as, if you accept the postulate that it is necessary to defend your country in war, you must recruit soldiers and compel them to fight when and where they are needed. The nineteenth-century industrialists hit on an efficient method of making the workers work. It was not, judged by more recent standards, a humane method. But it is difficult to see by what more humane method the end could have been achieved. Something can even be said for Townsend's view that labour under legal compulsion is never likely to produce " good and acceptable service ", and that " free " labour has its advantages even when the freedom consisted only in freedom to choose between starvation, the early nineteenth-century workhouse and the early nineteenth-century factory. Let us at any rate give the devil his due.

The method was worked out empirically by hard-headed practical men. The rationalization was worked out later, and fitted into the general philosophy of *laissez-faire*. Society had no call to intervene in the workings of the economic order — or rather had a duty not to intervene — precisely because those workings resulted (to use once more Macaulay's words quoted in the previous lecture) in conferring on " industry and intelligence " the " natural reward " of prosperity, and on " idleness and folly " the " natural punishment " of poverty. Just as the *entrepreneur* who was worsted in competition with his rivals was thereby proved to have been inferior to them in intelligence or application and thus deserved the misery and dishonour of the bankruptcy court, so the worker who failed to maintain himself in rivalry with his fellow-workers was *ipso facto* convicted of laziness and folly and justly condemned to the penalties of poverty and squalor. If the possession of wealth was the reward of virtue, vice was the explanation of poverty. As Tennyson remarked in one of his dialect poems, " the poor i' the loomp is bad ". The inscrutable workings of providence could thus be vindicated. " To make society happy ", as Mandeville had said, " it is necessary that great numbers should be wretched as well as poor " ; and this hypothesis was rendered tolerable by the assumption that they were poor because they were bad. Social stability rested on the unspoken belief that there would always be enough bad, and therefore poor, people to make the wheels go round. Perhaps today the authorities of countries which rely extensively on penal labour for public works sometimes similarly congratulate themselves on the fortunate dispensation of providence which keeps up the supply of criminals.

Broadly speaking, the system of labour incentives thus established remained intact, together with the rest of the *laissez-faire* mechanism, till the end of the nineteenth century. Protective action to mitigate its harshness was not extensive enough to throw the machine out of gear. Less brutal pressures were required to maintain established habits of work than had been required to establish them in the first instance. Early humanitarian legislation was directed to improve conditions of work in factories and mines. Mitigation of the harshnesses of the poor law and its administration came much later, so that the conspicuous gap between the lesser evil of factory life and the greater evil of the poor law and its workhouse was maintained to deter the work-shy. The stigma of receiving public assistance was deeply imprinted in the Victorian moral code ; so advanced a reformer as J. S. Mill recoiled in horror from the idea that anyone in this disgraceful situation should have a vote. Nevertheless, as the nineteenth century went on, this part of the philosophy of *laissez-faire* became increasingly vulnerable. In the 1880's Charles Booth conducted his great investigation of poverty in the London slums ; in the next decade Rowntree made his more detailed survey on a smaller scale in York. The rapid expansion of social services after the Liberal victory of 1906 was the symptom of an altogether new climate of opinion. By 1914 it was no longer seriously possible to equate poverty with vice or to believe that the poor deserved to be poor as the " natural punishment " of their own short-comings. Poverty, diagnosed as a social disease, could no longer be regarded as an indispensable element in a healthy economy. The labour philosophy of *laissez-faire* had been turned inside-out.

This transformation did not arise simply from the growth of humanitarian sentiment or of the social conscience. Like other factors which brought about the decay of *laissez-faire* capitalism, it arose directly from the forces making for con-centration within capitalism itself. Just as the capitalists, instead of competing against one another as isolated indi-viduals, began to form larger and larger combines in order to increase their efficiency and strengthen their bargaining power, so for exactly the same motives the workers began to group themselves into larger and larger trade unions. The individual *entrepreneur* hiring and firing individual workers was replaced by the big concern negotiating collective labour contracts with a big trade union. The same cry which was raised against monopoly was raised more raucously and more persistently against the trade unions. The basis of the protest was the same : the trade union, like the monopolist, was substituting group solidarity for unlimited competition between individuals. Just as a manufacturer joined a cartel or bound himself by a written or unwritten price agreement not to undersell his fellow-manufacturers or poach on their markets, the essence of the trade union was that its members should not bid against one another on the labour market. Human beings refused to compete against one another to the point of exterminating the less fit and less efficient for the hypothetical good of the whole community ; and this refusal played havoc with an economic system based on the principle of automatic rewards for virtue and automatic penalties for sloth.

These developments were gradual and piecemeal. Unorganized workers survived side by side with small businesses. Trade unions themselves were often small and found it difficult to combine with one another. Broadly speaking, before 1914 the trade union was still no match for the industrialist in bargaining power. The days when the individual worker was completely at the mercy of the individual employer were long past. But the trade union negotiators could still not afford to drive too hard a bargain with the managing director of the big company. The company was able to wait ; the men would be on the streets faced with starvation once the slender funds of the union were exhausted. Fear of hunger was still a real incentive. Even with the growth of large-scale organization on the side both of industry and of labour, the worker was still driven to work, as he had been driven for a century past, by what Ernest Bevin many years later was to call " the most unfortunate discipline of all, the economic whip ".

The widespread revolt against the fear of hunger as the incentive of labour and the " economic whip " as the instrument of discipline is barely twenty years old, and we are only just beginning to understand the magnitude of the achievement and the magnitude of the new problems which it creates. Here, too, mass unemployment was the decisive historical factor in the downfall of the *laissez-faire* economy. The wave of unemployment in Great Britain after the South African war was a crucial turning point. For the first time it became clear beyond any possibility of error or disguise that the disaster of unemployment and poverty was in no sense whatever a penalty for idleness or incompetence, that it fell like God's rain equally on the just and on the unjust, and that its causes were far profounder than any individual could alter or even accurately diagnose. In 1909 a young social worker named Beveridge published a book called *Unemployment — a Problem of Industry* : the title itself was a novelty and a challenge. After the first world war, the mass unemployment of the early 1920's and the great depression of the early 1930's drove home all the old lessons and added a new one : unemployment was a problem not only of industry but of society. Two bitter phrases which attained universal currency — " the dole " and " the means test " — recall the controversies of the period. But the great depression finally won general acceptance in Britain for the view that, in work or out of work, the adequate maintenance of the worker was a public obligation. The structure of the welfare state began to rise on the foundations laid by Lloyd George twenty years before. The second world war stimulated the process. In 1944 the Coalition Government solemnly announced in a White Paper that they " accept as one of their primary aims and responsibilities the maintenance of a high and stable level of employment after the war ". The Labour Government after 1945 took over this obligation and added fresh stones to the already impressive edifice of social services. Details of the structure have been sharply criticized by the Opposition. But its main pillars — full employment, the health services and the food subsidies — have all received explicit Conservative endorsement. So far we have come on the road to the welfare state.

The transition from the " economic whip " to the welfare state is, however, bringing its embarrassments. Critics of the welfare state argue that the enjoyment of social services and higher standards of living will weaken the initiative and independence of the worker. It is the precise contrary which is true. What the nineteenth-century employer feared was that too much assistance and too much prosperity for the worker would make him more, not less, independent and self-reliant, and therefore less amenable to the discipline of industry. This is the danger today. Before the second world war it had been remarked how immensely the bargaining power of the trade unions had been increased by the knowledge that the unemployed would now be supported out of public funds and not, as formerly, out of the reserves of the unions themselves. The combination of the welfare state with full employment tends to put the worker in a position where he may feel that he has everything to gain and hardly anything to lose. Such conditions prepare the way for an upward pressure on wage-rates, which may easily become irresistible in a period of rising prices and increasing strains on the standard of living.

It is a disquieting and unhealthy symptom of our contemporary social situation that this crucial question seems to be generally enveloped in a conspiracy of silence. It is raised only by the die-hards ; willingness to discuss it at all generally goes with a nostalgic longing to return to the world of hiring and firing and the economic whip. " Critics of the Beveridge report ", wrote a well-known financier in a letter to *The Times* when that report was presented at the end of 1942, " say that fear of starvation is a stimulus." The same hypothesis is more prudishly expressed in the view, frequently heard before rearmament began, that our troubles would be solved by a dose of unemployment. Of course, this is perfectly true. Let us not be squeamish about these things. Of course, fear of starvation is a stimulus ; the whole nineteenth century proved that. Of course, the prevalence of unemployment promotes discipline in the factories. The point about these sanctions is not that they are ineffective, but that they are today unacceptable in any enlightened society and unenforceable except in conditions which will ultimately destroy the social fabric. They belong to a kind of society which is rapidly passing into history. Those who seek to maintain or revive them are merely keeping their eyes strained towards the ruins on the shore that lies behind us.

The widespread survival of this mood among the former ruling and privileged groups has a logical and extremely serious consequence. It encourages the survival of a similar mood among the workers. They also spend too much time looking back — not, indeed, eagerly, but anxiously — towards the ruins ; they also are preoccupied with the outlook of the *laissez-faire* world of the past. And this happens for two reasons.

In the first place, the workers have learned only too well the lessons taught them by their betters in the nineteenth century. They learned from the theologians that work is a curse imposed on man by the Fall ; they learned from the economists that work is a " disutility " to be suffered only in order to obtain a greater good or avoid a greater evil, and that labour power is a market commodity whose price fluctuates in accordance with the laws of supply and demand. The cynical doctrine that the individual could and should be moved by considerations of self-interest and that these were identical with his duty to society has been inherited from the employer by the worker. The elimination of the old incentive of fear of hunger and unemployment will not automatically persuade him to abandon the time-honoured view of his relations with the employer as a hard-fought bargain at the moment when the bargaining conditions have turned so dramatically in his favour. If he is now reproached with behaving selfishly, he can reply that that is how he has been taught to behave. For more than a hundred years he has learned to believe that men work only in order to win material awards or avoid material penalties and not for any conscious purpose related to the welfare of the society of which they are members. From this point of view, strikes and go-slow and absenteeism are perfectly legitimate uses of the economic whip by the worker against the employer —

as legitimate as the economic whip of hunger and privation formerly wielded by the employer against the worker. The worker has some reason to feel that the bosses — the employers, the government and the ruling class generally — are trying to change the rules of the game just at the moment when he has at last learned the rules well enough to turn them to his own advantage.

Secondly, the workers are less impressed than I am by the belief that the old world of hiring and firing, of the incentive of hunger, of the economic whip is really dead. Perhaps, indeed, I have been too optimistic in my prognostications. Perhaps the ship, having pushed off on the voyage towards the welfare state, will after all drift back to the shore it seemed to have left for good, and come to harbour once more among the ruins of the past. Certainly the repeated promises, not only of the government, but of all parties, to maintain policies of full employment have carried something less than conviction among the workers, who have vivid memories of unemployment in the past and keen fears of unemployment in the future. Is it possible that this scepticism is justified? Can the promises really be relied on? Those who look round can find disquieting symptoms. Widespread unemployment exists today both in Germany and in Italy under the very eyes of the Allied authorities. Did the British Government ever go on record as protesting against the policies which allowed this situation to arise, supposing that it could not prevent them? Even in Britain can we be sure that the present or some future government will always be strong enough to resist demands which, if satisfied, would make unemployment inevitable? Suppose shortages of raw materials brought a threat of unemployment, can we be sure that the occasion would not be welcomed and even hastened by those who preach a dose of unemployment as the key to discipline in the factories? Questions like these lie behind many present anxieties. We need not put a sentimental halo round the industrial workers. Some of them — though probably not more than in other sections of the community — are taking things a lot too easily. Some of them are making hay while the sun shines — under the impression that it may not shine very long. But there is still a great deal to be lived down in the way of resentments from the past and fears for the future. Fear of unemployment, doubt whether we have yet really turned our back on the methods of the past — these are the most serious obstacles of all on the side of the workers in the way of the approach to the new society.

These recriminations are salutary because it is necessary to understand why the workers do not at the present time respond very readily to exhortations from employers, Government spokesmen, clergymen and trade union leaders to take a higher view of their obligations to society. But recriminations, though sometimes salutary, are never constructive ; and it is important that, having got through the mutual mud-slinging, we should take stock and attempt to discover where we stand.

The sum of what has happened since the dawn of the present century has not only destroyed one of the well-laid foundations of the Industrial revolution, but is bringing us back to once familiar and universally accepted doctrines : first, that society has an obligation to provide a decent standard of life for all its members ; and second, that society has an obligation to provide useful or productive work within their capacity for them to perform. But the turn of the wheel has not yet reinstated the third doctrine which is a necessary corollary of the other two — that society has both an obligation and a right to see that they perform that work. This reinstatement has become essential. " You cannot have social security in this country ", said Mr. Bevin in a speech in the House of Commons in 1943, " without having some obligation." Yet it would be foolish to pretend that a return to conceptions of social obligation prevalent before the

Industrial revolution can take the form of a mere restoration of the *status quo ante*. A century of history cannot be simply wiped out. The social habits and labour incentives of the pre-industrial period cannot be resumed. But all that we have yet succeeded in doing is to destroy the philosophy, habits and incentives which for a century past have made the wheels of industry turn, without putting anything in their place. The task ahead is nothing less than the creation of a new philosophy which will furnish an incentive and a reinforcement for a new social habit of work.

The first and most obvious incentive suggested is to increase the share of the worker in the proceeds of his work. Humane people who recognize that the " economic whip " of hunger and unemployment has become intolerable and unacceptable, but are yet reluctant to abandon the foundation of economic motive on which the *laissez-faire* philosophy rests, take refuge in the idea of substituting the positive inducement of higher economic rewards for the negative deterrent of economic penalties. It is true enough that men who enjoy higher wages and therefore a higher standard of living are on the whole capable of more productive work than those in lower grades. It is also true that generous piece-rates can stimulate production, at any rate for a time. But when we pass beyond the limited scope of these observations, the fallacy of believing in higher wages as a main incentive to replace fear of want becomes quickly apparent.

The consequences of this phenomenon lie not far beneath the surface. Fear of want is so fundamental, so animal, a force that it possesses a driving-power different not merely in degree, but in its sheer elemental nature, from that of any more refined economic motive ; and the promoters of the system of private enterprise were perfectly right in treating it as the only adequate incentive for which a place could be found in their philosophy of economic self-interest. The lure of higher wages has none of this universal driving-power.

The man who finds his earning power enhanced by higher wages may prefer to take the benefit in the form not of increased income, but of increased leisure — perhaps for himself, perhaps for his wife and children, who need no longer be sent out to work, so that rising wages may even be reflected in falling production. While the desire to avoid hunger is a universal human motive, the desire for a higher standard of living, once a conventional level of subsistence has been reached, is perhaps the exception rather than the rule. The stimulus to production obtainable from higher rewards is at best a wasting asset.

The second group of remedies designed to revive the flagging labour incentive is directed not to the remuneration but to the status of the worker. The establishment of works councils with powers over matters of discipline as well as organization, access by the workers' representatives to production costs and balance-sheets, representation of workers on the board, profit-sharing and co-partnership schemes, and many similar devices have been tried or advocated. The general verdict is that they are good as far as they go without going very far. Improved working conditions and greater opportunities of consultation between management and workers are always welcomed and allay discontent; but they have little positive result in creating fresh incentives or in making the worker feel that the success of the enterprise is a matter of personal concern to himself and has a moral claim on his most efficient service. A certain element of make-believe attending all such efforts is revealed in the slogan " industrial democracy " sometimes applied to them. Everyone, workers included, knows that an industrial concern cannot be run by methods of democratic control; and the kind of democracy meant resembles at best that formerly adopted in crown colonies where the nominated representatives of the governor outvoted the elected representatives of the people on any vital issue.

The third source from which a new incentive for labour might be derived is the nationalization of industry, which represents the conception of industrial democracy on the national plane rather than on that of the particular factory or industry. This is a more real and more substantial proposition. The essence of so-called private enterprise, even when it takes the form of large-scale monopoly or oligopoly, is that it is capable of making only an economic appeal to the worker. Its practice and aim is profit-earning; its philosophy of work recognizes material gain as the sole effective stimulus. Once it departs from this premise, it becomes a public utility and had better be recognized and organized as such. It is true that, as has often been observed, the attitude of workers in state or municipal undertakings or in public corporations has never been, and is not today, notably different from that of workers for private enterprises. But this is scarcely a relevant argument. The workers know quite well that the national economy, so far as major decisions of policy go, is a single entity; and in Great Britain it is not yet the nationalized sector which dominates industrial policy. We have not yet invited the worker to work in a society in which he is a full and equal partner and takes his full part in the running of affairs, including the management of its industries and its economic policy. My inclination is to believe that the nationalization of the major part of industry would be a necessary condition of the transition from purely economic incentives to incentives which include a sense of social obligation on the part of the worker; and I would add this to the reasons advanced in the previous lecture why, in the predicament at which we have arrived, we have to advance towards socialism as there defined — or perish. But while this may be a condition precedent of the solution of our problem, it does not by itself provide a solution; and it is not my purpose to gloss over the basic difficulty of labour incentives under any kind of socialist order.

It is common in discussions of this subject to speak of " work " as if it were just work, exactly as in discussions of international trade we speak of " imports " and " exports " as if the things we buy and sell were just imports and exports. Of course, work is not just work. Delivering these lectures is, from my point of view, work. Engineers are controlling and manipulating the devices which carry my voice to you : that is work. People are sitting in offices, writing on papers and sorting them : that is work. People are driving lorries or minding machines or selling things in shops ; people are digging the land or hewing coal, or laying bricks or collecting garbage : all that is work. Innumerable other forms of occupation are work in the technical sense of something by doing which you get your livelihood. Now it might be possible to get general assent to the proposition that every citizen has an obligation to work for the society of which he is a member and whose benefits he enjoys, and even for the proposition that refusal to work would incur penalties. But it is a long step from acceptance of these general principles to acceptance of the specific proposition that John Smith should be obliged under penalties to lay bricks or to dig the land, and Betty Jones to mind a machine or scrub a hospital floor. Yet it is beyond dispute that these tasks — and thousands of others — are tasks which society must have performed for it, if it is to survive at all. The question is not simply in general terms how to make people work, but how to fit specific individuals in the right proportions to specific jobs, and to get the jobs efficiently done. This the *laissez-faire* private enterprise capitalist system achieved by what Townsend called " the peaceable, silent, unremitting pressure " of hunger. A new society which has forsworn that means of pressure must find other means equally effective to achieve the same end.

Let us begin by admitting that few of us ever stop to reason or reflect about the incentives which make us work. The work we do has become a normal social habit, and it would be intolerable if every day or every week we paused on our way to the office or the factory to ask ourselves why we were doing it. Nevertheless, it is the incentives consciously or unconsciously recognized as valid which determine the social pattern; without them the pattern will gradually fade and disintegrate. What is happening around us at the present time is that the incentives of the old order have run down, that the habit of work is deteriorating and that the incentives of the new society have not yet been created. It would be absurd to deny that man needs to work, that he derives from work a satisfaction which he can get from nothing else, and that this satisfaction can be derived from any kind of work, however arduous, however tedious and however apparently distasteful in itself, provided it is felt to have a meaning and to serve a purpose. Indeed, I suspect that the differences in satisfaction derived by different individuals from different kinds of work are due far more to temperamental differences between the individuals than to objective differences between the work done by them. But it is an illusion to suppose that human nature in itself provides a stimulus to work of a kind which will secure the performance of the tasks necessary to the existence of society. All that human nature does is to provide material which is capable of responding to external incentives of sufficient cogency and vigour.

The incentives required are of two kinds — positive and what I will tremblingly and delicately call negative. As we have seen, increased rewards, increased inducements, are not enough. In two words, the donkey needs to see the stick as well as the carrot. I suppose I have been more fortunate than most people in being able to choose congenial jobs. I have often worked because I wanted to, and often because of something I wanted to get; but, if I am frank with myself, I have also sometimes worked because, if I had stopped working, the consequences for me would have been in one way or another disagreeable. I suspect that, if we examine our hearts, that is true of everyone. Everyone has mixed motives; and, in that queer conglomeration of conscious, half-conscious and unconscious impulses which drive us to work, I believe that desire to avoid unpleasant consequences is always one element. The provision of positive incentives to work in the new society will not be an easy task. But the most difficult task of all is to devise the ultimate and final sanction to replace the ultimate sanction of hunger — the economic whip of the old dispensation. Moreover, in a society which rightly rejects the pretence of separating economics from politics and denies the autonomy of the economic order, that sanction can be found only in some conscious act of society. We can no longer ask the invisible hand to do our dirty work for us.

I confess that I am less horror-struck than some people at the prospect, which seems to me unavoidable, of an ultimate power of what is called direction of labour resting in some arm of society, whether in an organ of state or of trade unions. I should indeed be horrified if I identified this prospect with a return to the conditions of the pre-capitalist era. The economic whip of *laissez-faire* indubitably represented an advance on the serf-like conditions of that period: in that relative sense, the claim of capitalism to have established for the first time a system of " free " labour deserves respect. But the direction of labour as exercised in Great Britain in the second world war seems to me to represent as great an advance over the economic whip of the heyday of capitalist private enterprise as the economic whip represented over pre-capitalist serfdom. Much depends on the effectiveness of the positive incentives, much, too, on the solidarity and self-discipline of the community. After all, under the system of *laissez-faire* capitalism the fear of hunger remained an ultimate sanction rather than a continuously operative force. It would have been intolerable if the worker had been normally driven to work by conscious fear of hunger ; nor, except in the early and worst days of the Industrial revolution, did that normally happen. Similarly in the society of the future the power of direction should be regarded not so much as an instrument of daily use but rather as an ultimate sanction held in reserve where voluntary methods fail. It is inconceivable that, in any period or in any conditions that can now be foreseen, any organ of state in Great Britain would be in a position, even if it had the will, to marshal and deploy the labour force over the whole economy by military discipline like an army in the field. This, like other nightmares of a totally planned economy, can be left to those who like to frighten themselves and others with scarecrows.

The attitude of the new society to work is perhaps the most crucial issue which it has yet to face, since the fate of every society depends in the long run on the productivity of its workers. Whatever may be true of the political rights of man, the economic rights of man are meaningless and valueless without the acceptance of correlative economic obligations. A society which undertakes to ensure freedom from want to its members must be able to count on keeping up a level of organized production sufficient to meet their basic needs. Yet on no issue is the transition from the conceptions of the old society to those of the new marked by more hopeless confusion. The *laissez-faire* view of wages as the price of labour has long been tempered by the principle of a minimum wage adjusted to need, by family allowances and by social insurance ; differences of remuneration originally designed to provide an incentive for the most intelligent and most industrious have been increasingly ironed out by the incidence of a highly progressive income tax ; and the whole structure has now been overlaid by the structure of the welfare state in flat contradiction with the original design of the edifice. And this fog of confusion about positive incentives is made thicker by almost total reluctance to face the necessity of some form of sanction for a direction of labour to take the place of the discarded — and rightly and necessarily discarded — economic whip. On no subject is discussion more urgently needed — and most of all among workers themselves ; for this is not a question which can simply be left to politicians, intellectuals or even trade union leaders. It will be difficult to provoke that discussion until more confidence has been gained that we have once for all cast aside our nostalgia for the economic whip, for the salutary dose of unemployment, for the ruins on the shore that lies behind ; and it will be difficult to conduct it in isolation from such other issues as the nationalization and management of industry. Nevertheless, no subject is more vital ; for, as Professor Hawtrey has said, " what differentiates economic systems from one another is the character of the motives they invoke to induce people to work ". This decision will do more than any other to determine the fate, and mould the shape, of the new society.

IV

FROM INDIVIDUALISM TO
MASS DEMOCRACY

THE problem of political organization in the new society is to adapt to the mass civilization of the twentieth century conceptions of democracy formed in earlier and highly individualistic periods of history. The proclamation by the French revolution of popular sovereignty was a serious challenge to institutions which had grown up under quite different auspices and influences. It is no accident that Athenian democracy, which has been commonly regarded as the source and exemplar of democratic institutions, was the creation and prerogative of a limited and privileged group of the population. It is no accident that Locke, the founder of the modern democratic tradition, was the chosen philosopher and prophet of the eighteenth-century English Whig oligarchy. It is no accident that the magnificent structure of British nineteenth-century liberal democracy was built up on a highly restrictive property franchise. History points unmistakably to the fact that political democracy, in the forms in which it has hitherto been known, flourishes best where some of the people, but not all the people, are free and equal; and, since this conclusion is incompatible with the conditions of the new society and repugnant to the contemporary conscience, the task of saving democracy in our time is the task of reconciling it with the postulate of popular sovereignty and mass civilization.

Modern democracy, as it grew up and spread from its focus in western Europe over the past three centuries, rested on three main propositions : first, that the individual conscience is the ultimate source of decisions about what is right and wrong ; second, that there exists between different individuals a fundamental harmony of interests strong enough to enable them to live peacefully together in society ; third, that where action has to be taken in the name of society, rational discussion between individuals is the best method of reaching a decision on that action. Modern democracy is, in virtue of its origins, individualist, optimistic and rational. The three main propositions on which it is based have all been seriously challenged in the contemporary world.

In the first place, the individualist conception of democracy rests on a belief in the inherent rights of individuals based on natural law. According to this conception, the function of democratic government is not to create or innovate, but to interpret and apply rights which already exist. This accounts for the importance attached in the democratic tradition to the rights of minorities within the citizen body. Decision by majority vote might be a necessary and convenient device. But individuals belonging to the minority had the same inherent rights as those belonging to the majority. Insistence on the rule of law, preferably inscribed in a written and permanent constitution, was an important part of the individualist tradition of democracy. The individual enjoyed certain indefeasible rights against the society of which he was a member ; these rights were often regarded as deriving from a real or hypothetical " social contract " which formed the title-deeds of society. Just as the individualist tradition in *laissez-faire* economics was hostile to all forms of combination, so the individualist tradition in politics was inimical to the idea of political parties. Both in Athenian democracy and in eighteenth-century Britain, parties were regarded with mistrust and denounced as " factions ".

The French revolution with its announcement of the sovereignty of the people made the first serious assault on

this view of democracy. The individualism of Locke's
" natural law " was replaced by the collectivism of Rousseau's " general will ". Both Pericles and Locke had
thought in terms of a small and select society of privileged
citizens. Rousseau for the first time thought in terms of
the sovereignty of the whole people, and faced the issue of
mass democracy. He did so reluctantly ; for he himself
preferred the tiny community where direct democracy,
without representation or delegation of powers, was still
possible. But he recognized that the large nation had come
to stay, and held that in such conditions the people could be
sovereign only if it imposed on itself the discipline of a
" general will ". The practical conclusion drawn from this
doctrine, not by Rousseau himself, but by the Jacobins, was
the foundation of a single political party to embody the
general will. Its logical conclusions were still more far-
reaching. The individual, far from enjoying rights against
society assured to him by natural law, had no appeal against
the deliverances of the general will. The general will was
the repository of virtue and justice, the state its instrument
for putting them into effect. The individual who dissented
from the general will cut himself off from the community
and was a self-proclaimed traitor to it. Rousseau's doctrine
led directly to the Jacobin practice of revolutionary terror.
It would be idle to embark on a theoretical discussion of the
rival merits of the two conceptions of democracy. Individualism is an oligarchic doctrine — the doctrine of the select
and enterprising few who refuse to be merged in the mass.
The function of natural law in modern history, though it
is susceptible of other interpretations, has been to sanctify
existing rights and to brand as immoral attempts to over-
throw them. A conception based on individual rights
rooted in natural law was a natural product of the oligarchic
and conservative eighteenth century. It was equally natural
that this conception should be challenged and overthrown

in the ferment of a revolution that proclaimed the supremacy of popular sovereignty.

While, however, the beginnings of mass democracy can be discerned in the doctrines of Rousseau and in the practice of the French revolution, the problem in its modern form was a product of the nineteenth century. The Industrial revolution started its career under the banner of individual enterprise. Adam Smith was as straightforward an example as could be desired of eighteenth-century individualism. But presently the machine overtook the man, and the competitive advantages of mass production ushered in the age of standardization and larger and larger economic units. And with the mammoth trust and the mammoth trade union came the mammoth organ of opinion, the mammoth political party and, floating above them all, the mammoth state, narrowing still further the field of responsibility and action left to the individual and setting the stage for the new mass society. It was the English Utilitarians who, by rejecting natural law, turned their backs on the individualist tradition and, by postulating the greatest good and the greatest number as the supreme goal, laid the theoretical foundation of mass democracy in Britain ; in practice, they were also the first radical reformers. Before long, thinkers began to explore some of the awkward potentialities of mass democracy. The danger of the oppression of minorities by the majority was the most obvious. This was discerned by Tocqueville in the United States in the 1830's and by J. S. Mill in England twenty-five years later. In our own time the danger has reappeared in a more insidious form. Soviet Russia has a form of government which describes itself as a democracy. It claims, not without some historical justification, to stem from the Jacobins who stemmed from Rousseau and the doctrine of the general will. The general will is an orthodoxy which purports to express the common opinion ; the minority which dissents can legitimately be suppressed. But we are not concerned here with the abuses and excesses of the Soviet form of government. What troubles us is the question how far, in moving from the individualism of restrictive liberal democracy to the mass civilization of today, we have ourselves become involved in a conception of democracy which postulates a general will. The question is all around us today not only in the form of loyalty tests, avowed or secret, or committees on un-American activities, but also in the form of the closed shop and of increasingly rigid standards of party discipline. In a speech made to a regional Labour party conference at the time of Mr. Aneurin Bevan's resignation in April, the Minister of Defence denounced "absence of loyalty" in the party: "The loyalty of our party", exclaimed Mr. Shinwell, "is superior to any exhibition of political private enterprise. . . . No person, I don't care who he is, can be allowed to interfere with the democratic structure of this party." Lenin used strikingly similar phrases at the Bolshevik party congress in March 1921. We have moved far from the conception of truth emerging from the interplay of divergent individual opinions. Loyalty has come to mean the submission of the individual to the general will of the party or group.

The second postulate of Locke's conception of society, the belief in a fundamental harmony of interests between individuals, equally failed to stand the test of time, and for much the same reason. Even more than natural law, the harmony of interests was essentially a conservative doctrine. If the interest of the individual rightly understood coincided with the interest of the whole society, it followed that any individual who assailed the existing order was acting against his own true interests and could be condemned not only as wicked, but as short-sighted and foolish. Some such argument was, for instance, often invoked against strikers who failed to recognize the common interest uniting them with their employers. The French revolution, an act of self-assertion by the third estate against the two senior estates of nobility and clergy, demonstrated — like any other violent upheaval — the hollowness of the harmony of interests ; and the doctrine was soon also to be powerfully challenged on the theoretical plane.

The challenge came from two quarters. The Utilitarians, while not making a frontal attack on the doctrine, implicitly denied it when they asserted that the harmony of interests had to be created by remedial action before it would work. They saw that some of the worst existing inequalities would have to be reformed out of existence before it was possible to speak without irony of a society based on a harmony of interests ; and they believed in increased education, and the true liberty of thought which would result from it, as a necessary preparation for establishing harmony. Then Marx and Engels in the *Communist Manifesto* took the class struggle and made out of it a theory of history which, partial though it was, stood nearer to current reality than the theory of the harmony of interests had ever done. Social and economic pressures resulting from the breakdown of *laissez-faire* illustrated in practice what Marx had demonstrated in theory. But in Great Britain it was reformist Utilitarianism rather than revolutionary Marxism that set the pace. The flagrant absence of a harmony of interests between competing and conflicting classes more and more urgently called for state intervention. The state could no longer be content to hold the ring ; it must descend actively into the arena to create a harmony which did not exist in nature. Legislation, hitherto regarded as an exceptional function required from time to time to clear up some misunderstanding or to rectify some abuse, now became normal and continuous. It no longer sufficed to interpret and apply rights conferred on the individual by the laws of nature. What was expected of the state was positive and continuous activity — a form of social and economic engineering. The substitution of a planned economy for *laissez-faire* capitalism brought about a radical transformation in the attitude towards the state. The functions of the state were no longer merely supervisory, but creative and remedial. It was no longer an organ whose weakness was its virtue and whose activities should be restricted to a minimum in the interests of freedom. It was an organ which one sought to capture and control for the carrying out of necessary reforms ; and, having captured it, one sought to make it as powerful and effective as possible in order to carry them out. The twentieth century has not only replaced individualist democracy by mass democracy, but has substituted the cult of the strong remedial state for the doctrine of the natural harmony of interests.

The third main characteristic of Locke's conception of society — a characteristic which helped to give the eighteenth century its nicknames of the Age of Reason or the Age of Enlightenment — was its faith in rational discussion as a guide to political action. This faith provided the most popular nineteenth-century justification of the rule of the majority as the basis of democracy. Since men were on the whole rational, and since the right answer to any given issue could be discovered by reason, one was more likely, in the case of dispute, to find right judgment on the side of the majority than on the side of the minority. Like other eighteenth-century conceptions, the doctrine of reason in politics was the doctrine of a ruling oligarchy. The rational approach to politics, which encouraged leisurely argument and eschewed passion, was eminently the approach of a well-to-do, leisured and cultured class. Its efficacy could be most clearly and certainly guaranteed when the citizen body consisted of a relatively small number of educated persons who could be trusted to reason intelligently and dispassionately on controversial issues submitted to them. The prominent rôle assigned to reason in the original democratic scheme provides perhaps the most convincing explanation why democracy has hitherto always seemed to flourish best with a restrictive franchise. Much has been written in recent years of the decline of reason, and of respect for reason, in human affairs, when sometimes what has really happened has been the abandonment of the highly simplified eighteenth-century view of reason in favour of a subtler and more sophisticated analysis. But it is none the less true that the epoch-making changes in our attitude towards reason provide a key to some of the profoundest problems of contemporary democracy.

First of all, the notion that men of intelligence and good will were likely by process of rational discussion to reach a correct opinion on controversial political questions could be valid only in an age when such questions were comparatively few and simple enough to be accessible to the educated layman. It implicitly denied that any specialized knowledge was required to solve political problems. This hypothesis was perhaps tenable so long as the state was not required to intervene in economic issues, and the questions on which decisions had to be taken turned on matters of practical detail or general political principles. In the first half of the twentieth century these conditions had everywhere ceased to exist. In Great Britain major issues of a highly controversial character like the return to the gold standard in 1925 or the acceptance of the American loan in 1946 were of a kind in which no opinion seriously counted except that of the trained expert in possession of a vast array of facts and figures, some of them probably not available to the public. In such matters the ordinary citizen could not even have an intelligent opinion on the question who were the best experts to consult. The only rôle he could hope to play was to exercise his hunch at the election by choosing the right leader to consult the right experts about vital, though probably still unformulated, issues of policy which would ultimately affect his daily life.

68

At this initial stage of the argument reason itself is not dethroned from its supreme rôle in the decision of political issues. The citizen is merely asked to surrender his right of decision to the superior reason of the expert. At the second stage of the argument reason itself is used to dethrone reason. The social psychologist, employing rational methods of investigation, discovers that men in the mass are often most effectively moved by non-rational emotions such as admiration, envy, hatred, and can be most effectively reached not by rational argument, but by emotional appeals to eye and ear, or by sheer repetition. Propaganda is as essential a function of mass democracy as advertising of mass production. The political organizer takes a leaf out of the book of the commercial advertiser and sells the leader or the candidate to the voter by the same methods used to sell patent medicines or refrigerators. The appeal is no longer to the reason of the citizen, but to his gullibility. A more recent phenomenon has been the emergence of what Max Weber called the " charismatic leader " as the expression of the general will. The retreat from individualism seemed to issue at last — and not alone in the so-called totalitarian countries — in the exaltation of a single individual leader who personified and resumed within himself the qualities and aspirations of the " little man ", of the ordinary individual lost and bewildered in the new mass society. But the principal qualification of the leader is no longer his capacity to reason correctly on political or economic issues, or even his capacity to choose the best experts to reason for him, but a good public face, a convincing voice, a sympathetic fireside manner on the radio ; and these qualities are deliberately built up for him by his publicity agents. In this picture of the techniques of contemporary democracy, the party headquarters, the directing brain at the centre, still operates rationally, but uses irrational rather than rational means to achieve its ends — means which are, moreover, not merely irrational but largely irrelevant to the purposes to be pursued or to the decisions to be taken.

The third stage of the argument reaches deeper levels. Hegel, drawing out the philosophical implications of Rousseau's doctrine, had identified the course of history with universal reason, to which the individual reason stood in the same relation as the individual will to Rousseau's general will. Individual reason had been the corner-stone of individualist democracy. Marx took Hegel's collective reason to make it the corner-stone of the new mass democracy. Marx purported to reject the metaphysical character of Hegel's thought. But, equally with Hegel, he conceived of history pursuing a rational course, which could be analysed and even predicted in terms of reason. Hegel had spoken of the cunning of reason in history, using individuals to achieve purposes of which they themselves were unconscious. Marx would have rejected the turn of phrase as metaphysical. But his conception of history as a continuous process of class struggle contained elements of determinism which revealed its Hegelian ancestry, at any rate on one side. Marx remained a thorough-going rationalist. But the reason whose validity he accepted was collective rather than individual.

Marx played, however, a far more important part in what has been called " the flight from reason " than by the mere exaltation of the collective over the individual. By his vigorous assertion that " being determines consciousness, not consciousness being ", that thinking is conditioned by the social environment of the thinker, and that ideas are the superstructure of a totality whose foundation is formed by the material conditions of life, Marx presented a clear challenge to what had hitherto been regarded as the sovereign or autonomous human reason. The actors who played significant parts in the historical drama were playing parts already written for them : this indeed was what made them significant. The function of individual reason was to identify itself with the universal reason which determined the course of history and to make itself the agent and executor of this universal reason. Some such view is indeed involved in any attempt to trace back historical events to underlying social causes ; and Marx — and still more Engels — hedged a little in later years about the rôle of the individual in history. But the extraordinary vigour and conviction with which he drove home his main argument, and the political theory which he founded on it, give him a leading place among those nineteenth-century thinkers who shattered the comfortable belief of the Age of Enlightenment in the decisive power of individual reason in shaping the course of history.

Marx's keenest polemics were those directed to prove the " conditioned " character of the thinking of his opponents and particularly of the capitalist ruling class of the most advanced countries of his day. If they thought as they did it was because, as members of a class, " being " determined their " consciousness ", and their ideas necessarily lacked any independent objectivity and validity. Hegel, as a good conservative, had exempted the current reality of the Prussian from the operation of the dialectic which had destroyed successively so many earlier historical forms. Marx, as a revolutionary, admitted no such absolute in the present, but only in the future. The proletariat, whose victory would automatically abolish classes, was alone the basis of absolute value ; and collective proletarian thinking had thus an objectivity which was denied to the thinking of other classes. Marx's willingness, like that of Hegel, to admit an absolute as the culminating point of his dialectical process was, however, an element of inconsistency in his system ; and, just as Marx was far more concerned to dissect capitalism than to provide a blue-print for socialism, so his use of the dialectic to lay bare the conditioned thinking of his opponents lay far nearer to his heart, and was far more effective, than his enunciation of the objective and absolute values of the proletariat. Marx's writings gave a powerful impetus to all forms of relativism. It seemed less important, at a time when the proletarian revolution was as yet nowhere in sight, to note his admission of absolute truth as a prerogative of the proletariat. The proletariat was for Marx the collective repository of Rousseau's infallible general will.

Another thinker of the later nineteenth century also helped to mould the climate of political opinion. Like Darwin, Freud was a scientist without pretensions to be a philosopher or, still less, a political thinker. But in the flight from reason at the end of the nineteenth century, he played the same popular rôle as Darwin had played a generation earlier in the philosophy of *laissez-faire*. Freud demonstrated that the fundamental attitudes of human beings in action and thought are largely determined at levels beneath that of consciousness, and that the supposedly rational explanations of those attitudes which we offer to ourselves and others are artificial and erroneous " rationalizations " of processes which we have failed to understand. Reason is given to us, Freud seems to say, not to direct our thought and action, but to camouflage the hidden forces which do direct it. This is a still more devastating version of the Marxist thesis of substructure and superstructure. The substructure of reality resides in the unconscious : what appears above the surface is no more than the reflexion, seen in a distorting ideological mirror, of what goes on underneath. The political conclusion from all this — Freud himself drew none — is that any attempt to appeal to the reason of the ordinary man is waste of time, or is useful merely as camouflage to conceal the real nature of the process of persuasion ; the appeal must be made to those subconscious strata which are decisive for thought and action. The debunking of ideology undertaken by the political science of Marx is repeated in a far more drastic and far-reaching way by the psychological science of Freud and his successors.

By the middle of the nineteenth century, therefore, the propositions of Locke on which the theory of liberal democracy were founded had all been subjected to fundamental attack, and the attack broadened and deepened as the century went on. Individualism began to give way to collectivism both in economic organization and in the forms and practice of mass democracy : the age of mass civilization had begun. The alleged harmony of interests between individuals was replaced by the naked struggle between powerful classes and organized interest groups. The belief in the settlement of issues by rational discussion was undermined, first, by recognition of the complex and technical character of the issues involved, later and more seriously, by recognition that rational arguments were merely the conditioned reflexion of the class interests of those who put them forward, and, last and most seriously of all, by the discovery that the democratic voter, like other human beings, is most effectively reached not by arguments directed to his reason, but by appeals directed to his irrational, subconscious prejudices. The picture of democracy which emerged from these criticisms was the picture of an arena where powerful interest-groups struggled for the mastery. The leaders themselves were often the spokesmen and instruments of historical processes which they did not fully understand ; their followers consisted of voters recruited and marshalled for purposes of which they were wholly unconscious by all the subtle techniques of modern psychological science and modern commercial advertising.

The picture is overdrawn. But we shall not begin to understand the problems of mass democracy unless we recognize the serious elements of truth in it, unless we recognize how far we have moved away from the conceptions and from the conditions out of which the democratic tradition was born. From the conception of democracy as a select society of free individuals, enjoying equal rights and periodically electing to manage the affairs of the society, a small number of their peers, who deliberate together and decide by rational argument on the course to pursue (the assumption being that the course which appeals to the majority is likely to be the most rational), we have passed to the current reality of mass democracy. The typical mass democracy of today is a vast society of individuals, stratified by widely different social and economic backgrounds into a series of groups or classes, enjoying equal political rights the exercise of which is organized through two or more closely integrated political machines called parties. Between the parties and individual citizens stand an indeterminate number of entities variously known as unions, associations, lobbies or pressure-groups devoted to the promotion of some economic interest, or of some social or humanitarian cause in which keen critics usually detect a latent and perhaps unconscious interest. At the first stage of the democratic process, these associations and groups form a sort of exchange and mart where votes are traded for support of particular policies ; the more votes such a group controls the better its chance of having its views incorporated in the party platform. At the second stage, when these bargains have been made, the party as a united entity " goes to the country " and endeavours by every form of political propaganda to win the support of the unattached voter. At the third stage, when the election has been decided, the parties once more dispute or bargain together, in the light of the votes cast, on the policies to be put into effect ; the details of procedure at this third stage differ considerably in different democratic countries in accordance with varying constitutional requirements and party structures. What is important to note is that the first and third stages are fierce matters of bargaining. At the second stage, where the mass persuasion of the electorate is at issue, the methods employed now commonly approximate more and more closely to those of commercial advertisers, who, on the advice of modern psychologists, find the appeal to fear, envy or self-aggrandizement more effective than the appeal to reason. Certainly in the United States, where contemporary large - scale democracy has worked most successfully and where the strongest confidence is felt in its survival, experienced practitioners of politics would give little encouragement to the idea that rational argument exercises a major influence on the democratic process. We have returned to a barely disguised struggle of interest-groups in which the arguments used are for the most part no more than a rationalization of the interests concerned, and the rôle of persuasion is played by carefully calculated appeals to the irrational subconscious.

This discussion is intended to show not that mass democracy is more corrupt or less efficient than other forms of government (this I do not believe), but that mass democracy is a new phenomenon — a creation of the last half-century — which it is inappropriate and misleading to consider in terms of the philosophy of Locke or of the liberal democracy of the nineteenth century. It is new, because the new democratic society consists no longer of a homogeneous closed society of equal and economically secure individuals mutually recognizing one another's rights, but of ill co-ordinated, highly stratified masses of people of whom a large majority are primarily occupied with the daily struggle for existence. It is new, because the new democratic state can no longer be content to hold the ring in the strife of private economic interests, but must enter the arena at every moment and take the initiative in urgent issues of economic policy which affect the daily life of all the citizens, and especially of the least secure. It is new, because the old rationalist assumptions of Locke and of liberal democracy have broken down under the weight both of changed material conditions and of new scientific insights and inventions, and the leaders of the new democracy are concerned no longer primarily with the reflexion of opinion, but with the moulding and manipulation of opinion. To speak today of the defence of democracy as if we were defending something which we knew and had possessed for many decades or many centuries is self-deception and sham.

It is no answer to point to institutions that have survived from earlier forms of democracy. The survival of kingship in Great Britain does not prove that the British system of government is a monarchy; and democratic institutions survive in many countries today — some survived even in Hitler's Germany — which have little or no claim to be called democracies. The criterion must be sought not in the survival of traditional institutions, but in the question where power resides and how it is exercised. In this respect democracy is a matter of degree. Some countries today are more democratic than others. But none is perhaps very democratic, if any high standard of democracy is applied. Mass democracy is a difficult and hitherto largely uncharted territory; and we should be nearer the mark, and should have a far more convincing slogan, if we spoke of the need, not to defend democracy, but to create it.

In my second and third lectures I discussed two of the basic problems which confront the new society — the problem of a planned economy and the problem of the right deployment and use of our human resources. These problems are basic in the sense that their solution is a condition of survival. The old methods of organizing production have collapsed, and society cannot exist without bringing new ones into operation. But those problems might conceivably be solved — are even, perhaps, in danger of being solved — by other than democratic means: here the task of mass democracy is to meet known and recognized needs by methods that are compatible with democracy, and to do it in time. The central problem which I have been discussing today touches the essence of democracy itself. Large-scale political organizations show many of the characteristics of large-scale economic organization, and have followed the same path of development. Mass democracy has, through its very nature, thrown up on all sides specialized groups of leaders — what are sometimes called élites. Everywhere, in government, in political parties, in trade unions, in co-operatives, these indispensable élites have taken shape with startling rapidity over the last thirty years. Everywhere the rift has widened between leaders and rank and file.

The rift takes two forms. In the first place, the interests of the leaders are no longer fully identical with those of the rank and file, since they include the special interest of the leaders in maintaining their own leadership — an interest which is no doubt rationalized, but not always justly, as constituting an interest of the whole group. The leaders, instead of remaining mere delegates of their equals, tend in virtue of their functions to become a separate professional, and then a separate social, group, forming the nucleus of a new ruling class or, more insidiously still, being absorbed into the old ruling class. Secondly, and most important of all, there is an ever-increasing gap between the terms in which an issue is debated and solved among leaders and the terms in which the same issue is presented to the rank and file. Nobody supposes that the arguments which the leaders and managers of a political party or a trade union use among themselves in private conclave are the same as those which they present to a meeting of their members ; and the methods of persuasion used from the public platform or over the radio will diverge more widely still. When the decision of substance has been taken by the leaders, whether of government, of party or of union, a further decision is often required on the best method of selling the decision. Broadly speaking, the rôle of reason varies inversely with the number of those

77

to whom the argument is addressed. The decision of the leaders may be taken on rational grounds. But the motivation of the decision to the rank and file of the party or union, and still more to the general public, will contain a larger element of the irrational the larger the audience becomes. The spectacle of an efficient élite maintaining its authority and asserting its will over the mass by the rationally calculated use of irrational methods of persuasion is the most disturbing nightmare of mass democracy.

The problem defies any rough-and-ready answer. It was implicit in Lincoln's formula of government " of the people " (meaning, I take it, belonging to the people in the sense of popular sovereignty), " by the people " (implying, I think, direct participation in the business of government) and " for the people " (requiring an identity of interests between governors and governed only obtainable when such participation occurs). It was implicit in Lenin's much-derided demand that every cook should learn to govern and that every worker should take his turn at the work of administration. The building of nineteenth-century democracy was long and arduous. The building of the new mass democracy will be no easier. The historian can here only look back over the way we have come, and analyse the fundamental questions which are being presented to the coming generation. He may be able to throw some light on the nature of the answers that are required ; but he cannot define or prescribe them.

For myself, it seems inconceivable that we can return to the individualist democracy of a privileged class ; and, by the same token, we cannot return to the exclusively political democracy of the weak state exercising only police functions. We are committed to mass democracy, to egalitarian democracy, to the public control and planning of the economic process, and therefore to the strong state exercising remedial and constructive functions. On the fundamental rôle of reason I shall say something in my last lecture. Here I will say only that I have no faith in a flight into the irrational or in an exaltation of irrational values. Reason may be an imperfect instrument ; and we can no longer take the simple view of its character and functions which satisfied the eighteenth and nineteenth centuries. But it is none the less in a widening and deepening of the power of reason that we must place our hope. Mass democracy calls just as much as individualist democracy for an educated society as well as for responsible and courageous leaders ; for it is only thus that the gap between leaders and masses, which is the major threat to mass democracy, can be bridged. The task is difficult but not hopeless ; and just as Great Britain has done more than any other country during the last five years to mark out new lines of social and economic advance, so I believe that she has better opportunities than any other country to lay the foundations of an educated mass democracy.

V

THE WORLD TRANSFORMED

THE conspicuous fact about the international scene today is the passing of power from western Europe : for the first time for many centuries western Europe is no longer the centre of the globe. Even our conventional geographical terminology has become obsolete and inappropriate. In a world whose focus of power is in Washington, our modern Far East lies somewhere in the countries of the so-called Iron Curtain, and our Far West along the eastern coast-line of Asia. The vast land mass of Europe and Asia located between these two lines has become a *terra incognita* almost impervious either to our military or to our missionary efforts, a territory no longer effectively belonging to our world at all, and resembling one of those no-man's-lands of early maps which the cartographers used to decorate with the comprehensive and sweeping inscription " Here be savages ".

The decay of Europe had long been heralded. It was confidently announced when the French revolution broke up the feudal structure of eighteenth-century Europe. Burke, in his famous *Reflections* on that event, announced that " the glory of Europe is departed ". In the 1820's Hegel, a philosopher whom it is not nowadays fashionable to quote except to condemn, called America " the land of desire for all those who are weary of the historical lumber-room of old Europe ", and " the land of the future where, in the ages that lie before us, the burden of the world's history shall reveal itself ". In the next decade Tocqueville, hailing the Russians and the Americans as the two great nations of the future, noted that " each of them seems to be marked out by the will of heaven to sway the destinies of half the globe ". At the end of the 1840's Alexander Herzen refused to believe that " the destinies and the future of humanity are fixed and nailed to western Europe ", and named the United States of America and Russia as the two young and vigorous nations which were preparing themselves to carry on the torch.

The prophecy, though brilliant, turned out to have been premature, and after the middle of the century was heard no more. Something very odd had happened. While the attention of political observers, theorists and enthusiasts was concentrated on the fate of the political revolution in France, another revolution — an Industrial revolution — had taken place in Great Britain, and, long before the Great Exhibition of 1851, which was its public advertisement, had transformed not only the face of Britain, but the face of the world. Some aspects of its political philosophy have been discussed in previous lectures. Here I have to deal with its international implications. The foundation of the Industrial revolution was steam-power, and Britain owed her leadership in it in part to the inventiveness and enterprise of her citizens and in part to her rich deposits of coal and iron. Its essence was a world-wide division of labour on an unprecedented scale. Steam-power made it economical to manufacture goods in larger quantities than the national market could absorb ; steam-power made it possible to transport them cheaply and rapidly to any part of the globe. Britain could become the manufacturing centre of the world ; in return for her manufactured goods the other countries could supply her with much-needed food and raw materials. After about 1870 the British manufacturing monopoly began to be seriously challenged, notably by Germany and the United States. But in a continually expanding market competition was little felt or feared ; and the system remained intact, though with a rapidly diminishing British preponderance, down to the end of the century. Throughout this period its wheels were oiled by the tactful financial management of the city of London. A world-wide money market and monetary system were kept in being, and equilibrium and discipline maintained by a carefully regulated flow of international investment, the main source of which was the British investing public.

Before the end of the nineteenth century the peculiar conditions which had created this remarkable and highly artificial type of world economy had begun to fade out. Its continuance depended on the possibility of progressive and relatively frictionless expansion by the leading industrial countries. In the 1880's competition for the few remaining vacant lots on the earth's surface was becoming acute. By 1900 new candidates, notably Japan and Russia, were jostling for a place in the charmed circle of industrial Powers. The final clash on a world scale came in 1914, and the magnificent and solid-seeming structure went down like a pack of cards. What was not recognized was that the nineteenth-century world economy was no longer a flourishing tree, but dying timber, when the hurricane struck it. The system of international division of labour and free (or relatively free) multilateral trading under the beneficent financial autocracy of the city of London had been a brilliant improvisation — so brilliant that to those who enjoyed its refreshing fruits it looked like lasting for ever. But some time before 1914 the trunk had begun to crumble, the rifts were visible ; and, once it was down, nothing could set it up again. The great illusion of the nineteenth century was not about the brilliant success of the social and economic order it created, nor about the contribution of that order to the wealth and welfare of mankind : these were, and are, unquestioned. The great illusion was that so transient and delicately poised a structure could be permanent — or even long-lived.

This illusion dominated the decade after the first world war. The overwhelming desire of the economic leaders of the victorious countries was to return to the " normalcy " of the halcyon days before 1914. The picture formed in their minds was of a world in which a natural and pre-established harmony had been broken, " barriers " were being wantonly put in the way of international trade, and the channels of international finance were needlessly and fatally " clogged ". Such a diagnosis was no doubt inevitable in countries which had been the main beneficiaries of the nineteenth-century world economy and among economists who had been bottle-fed on the immutable, though sometimes harsh, laws of political economy. But the politicians who saw through the illusions of the economists had no reason to congratulate themselves ; for they fell victims to the equally serious illusion that it was possible to return to the " normal " pre-1914 system of great nation-states resting on a balance of power maintained by a constant process of diplomatic bargaining. This was the international version of the liberal-democratic notion of government by compromise and by respect for the rights of minorities. It was the most serious and the most respectable of the illusions which paved the road to Munich. But with the new century the frontier had been closed ; frictionless expansion was no longer even a dream ; the presuppositions of the nineteenth-century order, political as well as economic, had collapsed. The illusion of harmony could no longer be re-created. Any prescription which presupposed a return to the old world economy or the old international balance of power was bound to fail.

What was left of the illusion of a return to the pre-1914 economic and political order was finally dispelled, over the greater part of the world, by the second world war. The United States of America alone provides a paradoxical exception to this process. The explanation of this anomaly is not far to seek. In the first place, the United States is still a young nation whose maturity came later than that of the principal European countries : it has taken much from Europe both in institutions and ideas, but often with a certain time-lag. Just as Woodrow Wilson came to Europe in 1919 speaking the language of Bright and Gladstone, so much of the climate of American economic and political opinion today recalls that of Britain in the 1920's, when concrete departures from economic orthodoxy had been undertaken, but orthodoxy itself was not yet seriously challenged, and when the supposed restoration of the European balance of power at Locarno was the major achievement of British foreign policy. Secondly, the blows of two world wars and the severest economic depression in modern history fell in the United States on a younger and less vulnerable economy than those of Europe. The crisis was acute and painful ; but, once it was over, the patient could believe that he had made a complete recovery, and did not, like his European brothers, regard the experience as the definitive end of a historical period. Thirdly, the nineteenth-century world economy, with its insistence on free competition, free exchanges and free access to markets, was the paradise of the economically strong, who wanted to enjoy the fruits of his strength without let or hindrance and resented the barriers thrown up by weaker countries in self-defence. Preponderant economic strength has now passed to the United States ; and it is extremely difficult for Americans to understand why policies which worked so successfully in the nineteenth century under British leadership should not work as well today under American leadership.

It has been repeatedly said — and not by Americans alone — that this is the American century in the same sense and with the same right as the last century was the British century. The torch of leadership has passed across the Atlantic. But is it not in essence the same torch ? Symptoms of such an assumption are apparent both in the economic and in the political spheres. Already before the second world war Cordell Hull saw himself as the twentieth-century Cobden ; during the war, in article 7 of the master lend-lease agreement, the Stars and Stripes were firmly nailed to the nineteenth-century mast-head of multilateral free trade ; after the war, the Bretton Woods agreement was a conscious American attempt to resuscitate the nineteenth - century international money - market. The new American diplomacy is directed to the establishment of an international balance of power in British nineteenth-century terms. It does not want to fight any more than nineteenth-century Britain wanted to fight ; it does not seek to conquer territory ; it does not seek to defend or promote an ideology. It wants to see power so comfortably balanced in Europe (and in Asia too) that it can leave Europe (and Asia) politically alone, and get on with the business of running the international economy. This is what — or so the text-books say — Great Britain achieved in the nineteenth century, and this is the wish-dream of American foreign policy ; and in order to realize this dream, support will be given to a nationalist Germany, to a semi-fascist Italy, to an avowedly fascist Spain, to a militarist Japan, and to all the most reactionary groups that can be found in the continent of Asia. There were periods in the past when Britain, in pursuit of the balance of power, could not afford to be ideologically fastidious about her alliances.

If, then, we want to understand American foreign policy — and it is an understanding which should give it every claim to our sympathy — we must realize that it is a partly conscious, partly unconscious imitation of British nineteenth-century achievement. Most Americans feel today that, with American leadership substituted for British leadership, the world could be as fine and peaceful and prosperous a place as it was a century ago (a little idealization of the past may come in here) if it were not for one untoward but incidental factor : the aggressiveness and intransigence of the Russians. They thus bitterly resent the intrusion of the Russians and of the Russian revolution as something which cheats them of their rightful heritage. Those feelings and opinions are perfectly natural. But the diagnosis on which they depend is dangerously lacking in historical perspective. To believe that the Russians are responsible for all the evil or all the difficulties in the world today is too easy an escape from our own responsibilities and tasks. We are steering our course on a stream of events whose head-waters can be traced in the broad historical region of the French, the American and the Industrial revolutions. The Russian revolution is a tributary which, joining the main river at a comparatively recent stage, has swollen it and made it more turbulent, but has probably not much deflected its course. The stream rolls on ; and it would still have been true without any Russian revolution that we are today navigating in very different waters, in a different landscape and a different climate from those through which we were passing in the mid-nineteenth century. If our new pilot tries to set his course by the same charts which served the old pilot well enough a hundred years back, he will be in serious danger of running the ship aground.

How, then, has the international scene changed fundamentally in the twentieth century ? In what respects are our nineteenth-century outlook and our nineteenth-century techniques now obsolete ? To sum up an infinity of detail under two broad heads, we are living today in a period of revolution which has now been in progress for nearly two centuries — what Marx would, I suppose, have called " permanent revolution " — and of which the two current phases may perhaps best be labelled the social revolution and the colonial revolution. Where do we stand in regard to these two world-wide revolutions ?

The main outlines of the social revolution have been described in previous lectures. It forms the transition from the " night-watchman " to the " social service " or " welfare " state — the state of which we demand that it shall bring about a larger measure of equality than ever before between its citizens — " fair shares for all " ; that it should as far as possible ensure both freedom and equality of opportunity for all ; that it should so plan and direct the national economy that the periodical crises inherent in *laissez-faire* systems should be avoided ; that full employment may be secured for all who are able to work, and that the natural resources and national man-power may be applied to the production of those things that are most needed, rather than of those things which can be sold at the highest profit ; and that it should so plan and direct our international trade that our scarce resources may be used to bring in those overseas supplies of which we are most in need, and on the most favourable terms. These are new and revolutionary functions for the state to perform, and the attempt to perform them will certainly bring with it many initial mistakes. But some comment is needed here on two international aspects of the contemporary social revolution — the Russian aspect and the American aspect.

The world being, in spite of the recent efforts of our diplomatic cartographers on both sides, all one place, the Russian revolution was a symptom and a part, though only a part, of the social revolution of the twentieth century. The social strains and stresses, which in the advanced industrial countries made themselves felt gradually and with comparative mildness, broke out with extreme violence in the most backward industrial country of all, thus falsifying the Marxist prediction that the proletarian revolution would occur where capitalism had reached its most mature development. The revolution of 1917, having occurred in backward Russia in the middle of the first world war, had to face the handicap, first of a primitive economy hopelessly shattered and dislocated by the impact of large-scale war, and, secondly, of a politically primitive community unused to any form of government save an unenlightened feudal autocracy. These conditions quickly infected the theory and practice of the revolution, which soon began to inspire horror and dismay even in circles that had at first greeted it with sympathy and enthusiasm. The attitude of Western countries towards the Russian revolution has been extraordinarily ambivalent. Sane judgment has always recognized that there was something in the Russian revolution to be learned as well as much to repel. But the proportion in which the two reactions should be blended has always been controversial. In part, divisions of opinion about it have been divisions between Right and Left. But in part also the division has been chronological, opinion having varied from period to period to match the changing state of relations between the Western countries and Soviet Russia. At the present moment these relations are notoriously worse than at any time in the past thirty years, and the current estimate of the Russian revolution stands at its lowest point. Indeed, it is now almost sufficient to discredit any policy to suggest that it bears some resemblance to something that has been done in Russia. This is a pity ; however human, it is a little childish to refrain from doing something that is desirable because our hated neighbours the Joneses have also found it desirable. From the point of view of socialism, it may well be a misfortune that the first socialist revolution should have occurred in a country with the political and economic background of Russia. But books written to show that if the British Government establishes a planned economy or nationalizes key industries, or controls foreign trade and exchange or the distribution of key commodities, or directs labour by the methods adopted during the war, then Britain is on the way to becoming a totalitarian police-state, are either disingenuous or rather silly. If one could add up the full account of the past thirty years, one might easily find that, so far as the countries of western Europe and America are concerned, more harm had been done by the bogy of communism in frightening people away from doing sensible things than had been done by communism itself.

The American aspect of our social revolution is more difficult. Reasons have already been suggested why the social revolution in the United States has lagged behind the social revolution in Europe — though less far in reality than public pronouncements would sometimes imply. The continued predominance of the principles of *laissez-faire* and private enterprise in the American economy — if in fact they do still predominate — would by itself cause no heart-burnings elsewhere. But these things are no longer safely exportable to the bleaker economic climate of Europe, where years of privation and unemployment have made large masses of people acutely conscious of social and economic inequalities, of extremes of wealth and penury existing side by side in the same society, of resources employed in the production of luxuries while basic needs go unsatisfied, and where there is general agreement on the necessity of using the machinery of the state to curb those evils of an unplanned and uncontrolled economy. As Mr. Alistair Cooke constantly reminds us in his admirable weekly broadcasts, America is not a country of big business men or of big men at all ; the vast majority of Americans are small people grappling with daily problems of making both ends meet, resentful of prices which have risen even more steeply than they have in Britain, and wanting to know what the Government are going to do about it. Perhaps it is a pity that the official voice of America does not reach Europe more often as the voice of the American little man. It would help to create a sense of greater solidarity across the Atlantic in facing comparable, if not identical, social problems, a sense of a common interest in our social revolution — by whatever name it may be called. Incidentally, it would be the best possible counter to the charge that American policy in Europe is more interested in the fate of big business than in the fate of the little man.

There is another point on which basic attitudes on the two sides of the Atlantic are apt to diverge : rearmament. Nobody in Europe denies the need for armaments. If American forces were withdrawn from Germany today as they were withdrawn from the 38th Parallel in Korea three years ago, a Korean incident would be likely to occur in Europe. I have never been a pacifist or questioned the importance of power in international affairs : it seems to me incontestable that, if the United States and the Western world were to disarm today, we should not have long to wait for substantial and catastrophic changes in the map of the world. But between this picture of total and helpless disarmament and a picture of all America and western Europe armed to the teeth and organized on a war footing, a line can be drawn ; and somewhere on this line the point of reason and common sense must be found. " War ", as Clemenceau said on a famous occasion, " is too serious a matter to be left to the generals " ; and this is a cold war, in which the home front is as important as the front line. The threat from Soviet Russia is not exclusively military. In many European countries underlying dissatisfaction with the hardships and inequalities of the social order creates vulnerable points, of which the widespread fear of communist parties, of fifth columns, of fellow-travellers and of infiltration into trade unions and other organizations provides clear evidence. Against these latent discontents rearmament is no security. The crux of the present situation is that, in the undamaged and still expansive economy of the United States, rearmament still means in large measure a using up of available resources, a taking up of the slack of surplus production, even a safeguard against potential unemployment. In Europe and in

Great Britain, on the other hand, rearmament means from the first moment a diversion of resources urgently needed for physical and social reconstruction, a fresh tightening of the belt, a further inroad on our social policies. In Great Britain in particular, our labour force is now barely sufficient to maintain the standard of living of a population whose age-structure is increasingly top-heavy. However generous American aid may be, the diversion of large numbers of able-bodied young men into the armed forces is bound to depress that standard still further. It is easy to imagine a point beyond which efficiency in the front line might be purchased at the cost of decreased stability and staying power on the home front. No decision facing the British Government — or European governments in general — today is more difficult or more important than this necessary balancing between military and social programmes. No point more urgently calls for American sympathy and understanding.

Here, then, is one of the two great forces which is transforming the face of twentieth-century politics and helping to mould the shape of the new society : the social revolution. The other is the colonial revolution. Here, too, we must start from an analysis of nineteenth-century society with its division of the world into advanced industrial and backward colonial peoples. This division of function, broadly corresponding with a division of colour, was the basis of the world economy ; racial inequality matched the inequality of economic status. Nor was this division seriously challenged till the new century opened. Then something began to stir. In 1900, at the time of the Boxer insurrection, the German Kaiser had spoken of the yellow peril and recommended his soldiers to behave like Huns. In January 1902 Great Britain, increasingly conscious, especially since the South African war, of the burden of world supremacy, broke all the rules by concluding alliance with a nation of the yellow race which had shown an astonishing aptitude in imitating the industrial techniques of the advanced Powers ; and in the same year a British economist, J. A. Hobson, published the first systematic analysis of economic relations between industrial and colonial nations, and gave a new and fruitful turn of meaning to the word which formed the title of his book *Imperialism*. The ruling group was displaying both material weakness and pangs of conscience — the usual prelude of revolution. The victory of Japan over Russia in 1905 resounded through Asia and through the world of coloured peoples. It was followed by the Russian revolution of 1905, the Persian revolution, the Turkish revolution and, most important of all, the Chinese revolution. It led to the first reforms which carried India along the road to self-government ; in Indonesia the first stirrings of revolt were heard against the paternalism of Dutch rule. After the first world war these movements grew in intensity and were supported by Soviet propaganda and sometimes by Soviet funds. But they required little fanning from outside ; nor were Soviet methods particularly successful. It was Japanese action in the second world war which brought the colonial revolution in Asia to a head. The emancipation of Asia from the white race was loudly proclaimed ; and after the victory it proved quite impossible to restore white supremacy, either military or economic, over the greater part of Asia. The movement has become a general revolt against political, economic and racial inequality ; colour is at least as important a factor as communism. The colonial revolution is not confined to Asia. It is on the march in Africa as well.

What is the character of this colonial revolution ? In the early years of the century, when the world was still dominated by the political presuppositions of *laissez-faire*, it expressed itself at first in political demands for the withdrawal of the capitulations in Egypt and Turkey, for self-government in India, for the abolition of the unequal treaties in China.

These political demands have not been abated. Everywhere today where the European nations still exercise any kind of political rule over " backward " peoples, the demand for political independence is more and more insistently raised ; and only where this demand has been unconditionally conceded, as in India, have relations between European and Asiatic peoples taken a turn for the better. The peoples of Asia, though divided among themselves by as many differences and mutual antagonisms as the peoples of Europe, are at present united in their desire to be rid of European political or military interference. Whatever acts of aggression may be committed in Asia, and whatever pronouncements may be made by the United Nations, it is important to realize that, from the Asiatic standpoint, any white armies fighting against Asiatic armies on the soil of Asia are *ipso facto* the aggressors. This view is common throughout Asia ; and any Asiatic nation or group which invokes or accepts the aid of European or American troops to fight against fellow Asiatics will be quickly branded as traitors to the common cause. This solidarity of Asia against white rule and white intervention is a new and rather frightening phenomenon. But here again we shall be mistaken if we regard the Soviet Union as a prime mover in these developments. In the present configuration of world politics, the Soviet Union profits from the clash between Asia and the Western world and will do everything to intensify it. But Russia did not create the colonial revolution, and cannot even now control its course. It might easily take lines unwelcome and embarrassing to Moscow if Western pressure were removed.

The underlying essence of the colonial revolution is today economic rather than political, and this gives the best hopes to the world of being able to weather it without disaster. The economic view of imperialism, promulgated by J. A. Hobson, by Lenin and by a host of other writers, has now thoroughly penetrated the consciousness of the leaders of the so-called backward peoples ; and they are turning against Europe the economic doctrines which they have learned from Europe, as they formerly did the political doctrines of Bright and J. S. Mill. What Asia and Africa are fundamentally in revolt against — whatever forms, political or economic, the revolt may take in day-to-day actions — is the nineteenth-century division of the world between advanced and backward peoples and the basis of that division in the intensive industrialization of certain areas of the world to the exclusion of others. Political independence and political equality are no longer enough. These achievements, which seemed all-important so long as they were out of reach, are now seen to be hollow and unreal unless they are backed up by the reality of economic independence and economic equality ; and the path to these is even longer and more difficult. The lesson has been thoroughly learned and digested that large-scale modern machine industry confers a high material standard of living and a widely diffused education and culture, as well as political and military power and prestige. Backward nations have been transformed into advanced nations through the process of industrialization — and in no other way. In the contemporary East, Gandhi's spinning-wheel is an obsolete cult. Industry is the symbol of progress. Imitation is the last and sincerest form of tribute paid by the colonial East to the industrial West.

The envy and admiration of the East for the achievements of the West, combined with a profound resentment of the inequalities of the past, make present relations complex and sensitive. Great Britain, conscious of a past to live down, seems for the moment more keenly aware of these difficulties than the United States, which in the past enjoyed prestige and popularity in Asia precisely because it held aloof from the interventionist policies of the European Powers. The nineteenth-century rôles of these two Powers in Asia have thus been in large measure reversed. The handicaps which the Western countries have to overcome in their Far Eastern policy are both political and economic. The handicap of political and military intervention which threatens to unite Asia against us must somehow be wound up ; the handicap of an economic tradition based on an unequal partnership for the division of labour must be lived down. We must face frankly the fact that our economic overtures will be received with suspicion. The suspicion will be due not so much to past experience as to the belief that the great industrial nations are unwilling for fear of competition to encourage industrialization on modern lines among the Asiatic peoples. This belief, fanned no doubt by interested parties, has figured prominently in recent propaganda where it has been alleged over and over again that the purpose of American bombing north of the 38th Parallel has been to destroy the rising industries of North Korea. The Chinese intervention in the Korean war appears to have been prompted in the first instance by apprehensions of attack on the power stations on the river Yalu which serve the industry of a whole region of Manchuria. Meanwhile the fact that the operations of the Washington Import-Export Bank and of President Truman's Point Four programme have hitherto been mainly directed to Latin America has helped to spread the fear that American economic and financial aid to under-developed countries may be dependent on the willingness of the recipient to come within the American sphere of political influence. These beliefs and these fears, ill-founded though they may have been, are a key to a highly sensitive point in the Asiatic policies of the Western Powers.

The colonial revolution advancing side by side with the social revolution and forming part of it, is the main reason why the world picture in the middle of the twentieth century is radically different than that of the nineteenth century. The nineteenth-century world economy was a coherent and highly integrated structure — artificial but efficient. The predominance of the industrial nations was unequivocally recognized; the development of the backward countries was carried out in a way, and at a pace, which suited their interests and satisfied their requirements. International trade flowed on lines which contributed most to the prosperity and greatness of the industrial countries. No question of a clash between advanced and backward nations could arise in what appeared to be a perfectly harmonious world: when the clash came it was between two advanced industrial nations, and the colonial peoples were objects of the dispute, not motive factors in it. The vast change that has come over our international society today is that the former backward peoples are no longer passive objects of policy, but driving forces. They have taken the initiative and placed the former great industrial Powers on the defensive. They have obtained recognition in principle of the doctrine of equal partnership. What has not yet been achieved is the translation of this doctrine into political and — still more important — into economic terms.

Here almost everything still remains to be done; and the urgent question is whether it can be done in time to stave off an explosion or to prevent the formation of a formidable anti-Western continental bloc stretching from the Elbe to the eastern seaboard of Asia. The issue has many analogies with that presented by the social revolution. Here, too, the main danger is the persistence of traditional ideas which have lost most of their validity in the contemporary world. In one respect an advance has been made. Nobody believes any longer that the development of Asia and Africa or the establishment of sound economic relations between them and the great industrial countries can be the work of private enterprise or private investment. Everyone recognizes that this is a case for initiative by governments. But is there not still some danger of governments themselves continuing to think in good nineteenth-century terms of regulating the development of backward countries by the needs of their own economies or of investing capital where it will earn the best return ? It is certain that Asia and the colonial countries will no longer be content to wait on the convenience of the Western economies. It is not altogether certain that capital investment is even the major requirement. The undeveloped countries are at once in possession of vast reserves of unused man-power. We do not yet know much — at any rate not nearly enough — about the conditions of the industrialization of backward territories in the twentieth century. Technical aid, and the planning and organization of their economies, are perhaps quite as necessary, and quite as likely to yield spectacular results, as the large-scale investment of foreign capital, particularly if this brings too many strings with it. One unhappy consequence of the present political situation is that China is unlikely to call in the aid of American and British technical advisers, who might in happier circumstances have played a capital rôle in the development of the new China and in building up relations between her and their own countries. Nor is the industrialization of the backward countries feasible without taking into account their economic relations with the rest of the world. A workable Chinese economy could conceivably be planned on a basis of self-sufficiency and internal markets. But this would not be conceivable for any of the other countries in question, and development would scarcely be possible if the new and struggling economy were to be placed at the mercy of a fluctuating and unprotected international market. Capital investment, technical aid, planned national economies, planned international trade — all these elements are necessary if the colonial revolution is to be guided to a successful and peaceful consummation. It would be a rash man who would undertake to arrange these four elements in order of importance. But it is certain that an attempt to operate with only one or two of them will end in frustration.

While the chief contemporary issues in international politics are intimately bound up with the social and colonial revolutions and cut across national boundaries, the most delicate question — and the one in which our diplomacy is most concerned — is that of relations between America and Europe. Of the many differences of outlook for which the broad Atlantic is mainly responsible, one is predominant in the present context. Americans, however much they shrink from war, are none the less able to look beyond a potential third world war to the prospect, however illusory, of peace regained, just as Europeans in the 1930's were still able to look beyond the potential second world war. Today Europeans know that little or nothing worth saving in Europe can survive a third war : they are not concerned, like many Americans, with the question how a third world war is to be won, but only with the question how it is to be avoided. And the fate that awaits Europe in the event of another war gives Europeans a far greater moral right to make their voices heard in international councils than could be claimed in virtue of their actual or potential contribution to the military strength of an alliance. In Professor Toynbee's brilliant epigram, " No annihilation without representation ".

But in what sense should Europe, and particularly Great Britain, make use of the right conferred on them by their grim stake in a third world war ? In what sense should we make our voice heard in Washington and New York ? In matters of rearmament there is not much that we can say except to plead that, besides armaments, there are other vital elements in our defences against communism which it would be dangerous to starve. But our main function must be continuously to make clear to American opinion, and to the American Government, that neither Europe nor Asia can return to the practices or precepts of the nineteenth-century order ; that, being unable to turn back, they are bound, if they would avoid sheer helplessness, to move forward along the line marked out by the social and colonial revolutions ; and that this advance is their best bulwark against the Soviet power. A healthy economy in Europe and a real independence in Asia would make the military task of defence modest and manageable. On the other hand, if we allow social inequalities and mass unemployment in Europe, and a refusal to recognize revolutionary national aspirations in Asia, to provide a rich field for Soviet propaganda, then the military task may well come to exceed our powers. That there is a serious possibility of any lasting or far-reaching agreement with Soviet Russia at the present time, I do not believe. But this makes it all the more important to look to our defences, and to recognize that the military part of those defences is not necessarily the most urgent and the most vital. The new world of Asia and much of the old world of Europe would welcome more active leadership from Great Britain in driving these points home in Washington. Like the responsibilities in domestic politics of which I have spoken in previous lectures, this responsibility is a difficult one for any British government to shoulder at a time when Britain's material situation in the world is relatively weaker than at any moment in the past two centuries. But the predicament of the world today is grave enough to make courage the highest form of prudence and the taking of risks the best insurance for ultimate security.

VI

THE ROAD TO FREEDOM

THE function of this last lecture is to draw together some of the threads which I have been spinning over the past five weeks and draw out the rudimentary pattern of some conclusions. The hope with which I embarked on these lectures — a hope not perhaps easily realizable in our time — was to be able to combine honesty and frankness with a measure of reasoned optimism for the future. It may be thought that I have passed too lightly over the possibility of catastrophe. Of that possibility I have throughout been intellectually conscious. But no society can live and function under the constant obsession of its own impending dissolution : the hypothesis of survival must be accepted, faith in the possibility of survival must exist, in order that society may be able to live and work for it. It may be thought that I have not dwelt with sufficient emphasis on the predicament in which we find ourselves. The gravity of that predicament I have no inclination to deny : what I wish to deny is that there is any predetermined pattern in history or pre-arranged destiny which condemns us to despair. As Lenin, who, being a good Marxist, was certainly not blind to the determinist elements in history, once remarked : " There is no situation from which there is absolutely no way out ". So much I would say with confidence of our present situation.

But this does not mean that every conceivable exit is open. The dilemma of free will and determination is logically inescapable. We are both free and not free. Time is short, and if we waste too much of it trying all the wrong exits we may well perish in the conflagration. The enquiry on which I have been engaged in these lectures rests on the belief that the study of history will help in the discovery which exits are available and which are not. The crisis has caught us — to revert to my old metaphor — in midstream. The fierce current which has borne us away from our moorings on the shore behind us is threatening to carry us down into the gulf. We can avoid disaster only if we bend all our efforts to navigate our ship towards the unknown shore in front. If too many of our crew are too much absorbed in nostalgic contemplation of the ruins on the backward shore, the navigation of the ship goes by default, and the prospect of our only means of escape is put in serious jeopardy.

Let me repeat, however, the *caveat* which I put forward in my first lecture, that no historical judgments are absolute and that any historical interpretation depends in part on the values held by the historian, which will in turn reflect the values held by the age and society in which he lives. It is therefore incumbent on the historian, whether explicitly or by implication, to make clear the values on which his interpretation rests, and this I shall attempt to do. But first let me contest an obvious criticism. Does not the admission that the values held by the historian necessarily enter into the history that he writes deprive history of any objective character? Can history in these conditions be more than a reflection of the whim of the historian? Now it seems to me foolish and misleading to deny the subjective element in history. Anyone who believes in the divine right of kings — a belief beyond the scope of argument — is bound to regard the last 150 years as a period of retrogression; and, if he is a historian of that period, he will weave his facts into a pattern of decline. But this does not mean that history is purely subjective. Life rejects these logical dilemmas of choice between opposites. The question of whether man is free or determined, like the famous question about the hen and the egg, permits of two contradictory answers, both equally valid. History is both subjective and objective. The historian takes his raw material, the dry bones of fact, and, articulating them under the inspiration of his own sense of values, turns them into the framework of living history. No metaphor can be fully appropriate or expressive, since any metaphor must be taken from the field either of science or art, and history is, properly speaking, neither science nor art, but a process containing some elements of both.

But, however much we may insist on the subjective element in history, we do regard objectivity as something towards which the historian should strive, even if he cannot fully attain it. In what sense, then, do we believe that history can become more objective? It is sometimes said that, with the development of mass civilization, the values which the historian brings to the study of history may tend to reflect less of personal idiosyncrasy and more of the conditions of his age and society, in other words, to become collective rather than individual values ; but, in so far as this change is real at all, I am not sure that the view of history through collective eyes is necessarily more objective than the view through the eyes of an individual. Then it is sometimes said that the improved techniques at the disposal of the historian for establishing his facts — notably the vast progress in statistical resources and methods — will make history more objective. The historian has reason to congratulate himself on far richer resources of all kinds than were enjoyed by his predecessors. He can, and should, write better history ; but, once again, I am not sure that this technical advance makes the function of interpretation any more independent of the values which the historian himself brings to it. Thirdly, I am myself tempted by the view that the historian's own greater consciousness of the subjective element in his work will help to make him more aware both of his own limitations and of the character of his own achievement. "Those historians who have no theory", observes Professor Hancock, "fill the vacuum with their prejudices." The most suspect historian is the one who makes the loudest professions of impartiality. The most objective historian on this view is the one who is most careful to check his own subjective interpretations by the equally subjective interpretations of others.

But in the long run I am not sure that we can wholly separate objectivity from belief in the truth of the values which we hold ; and this makes it all the more incumbent on me to examine some of the pre-suppositions which I have brought to the subject of these lectures and which have no doubt contributed to my interpretations and conclusions. The first relates to the rôle of reason in human affairs. In speaking of the flight from reason as an element in the transition from individualism to mass democracy, I referred to the influence of Marx and Freud. Both these thinkers were rationalists : they did not dethrone reason itself, but appealed from the over-simplified view of reason taken in the eighteenth and nineteenth centuries to a subtler and more sophisticated analysis. Other nineteenth-century thinkers went further in their assault on reason. Kierkegaard was perhaps the first who, by way of reaction against Hegel's exaltation of a rational reality, depicted man as a lonely and helpless figure planted in the midst of an irrational external world ; and the sudden and belated popularity of Kierkegaard's doctrines a century after they were first formulated is a tribute to our preoccupation with this most profound of all the problems of our contemporary mass society. Dostoevsky carried the revolt against reason from the philosophical to the ethical and political plane by making the rational morality of the Utilitarians the central target of his attack. The Utilitarians believed that man could be made moral by appealing to his rational sense of his own interest. For Dostoevsky man was in revolt against the tyranny of reason and dominated by the impulse to sin against his own interest; rational conviction could provide no bulwark against evil. Such a belief, transferred to the political world, clearly made nonsense both of political freedom and of political democracy. "To begin with unlimited freedom is to end with unlimited despotism", declares one of the characters in Dostoevsky's novel *The Devils*. To deny the validity of reason is to reject any form of government based on the hypothesis of rational discussion followed by a counting of heads. Democracy in any shape or form has no meaning or validity for Dostoevsky. He provides the best possible negative proof that a belief in reason is a prerequisite of belief in democracy.

Both Kierkegaard and Dostoevsky, as well as many others who have followed in their wake, drew the same conclusion from their diagnosis of the fundamental irrationality of the external world and of human nature: the leap into religion. Kierkegaard, having dwelt on the helplessness of the individual, preached the mystical union of the individual soul with God, thus saving the autonomous individual but merging him in a divine infinity. Dostoevsky believed that freedom and salvation could be attained only by the individual who merged himself in the community of the Orthodox Church, the Catholic Church having already become an instrument of reason and therefore of tyranny; the Orthodox Church and the Russian autocracy based on it provided the only foundation for a stable and ordered society. A third great thinker, Nietzsche, travelled the same path as Dostoevsky to a different and more logical conclusion. Having exposed the hollowness of all reason, of all democracy, of all conventional morality, he equally rejects the leap into religion of Kierkegaard and Dostoevsky. Nietzsche follows the path till he reaches a complete and absolute nihilism never perhaps achieved before or since in human thinking. Human action is deprived not merely of any rational motive but of any super-rational motive. It becomes simply the expression of a biological urge to self-assertion ; the will to power. Standing beyond good and evil, and recognizing no conscious ultimate purpose, Nietzsche's superman is the perfect animal. Nietzsche is at the opposite pole to those who subordinate means to ends and hold that the end sanctifies the means. He believes only in action as a good in itself without reference to ends. The political thinker who took most from Nietzsche was the syndicalist philosopher Sorel who preached the myth of the general strike as a value in itself, and declared " that the movement is everything, the goal nothing ". Mussolini proclaimed himself a pupil of Sorel. But neither Fascism nor Nazism was in true Nietzschean tradition. The glorification of the state or the nation in which they indulged would have seemed to Nietzsche quite as vulgar and bogus as the bourgeois ideals of liberal democracy.

Nietzsche is an important thinker because he alone carried the revolt against reason to its ultimate limit, and thus provided the proof — once more a negative proof — that man, when he cuts adrift from reason, denies his own nature and is lost. But when today we reassert our belief in reason, we can no longer accept much that was commonly accepted in the nineteenth century. We can no longer believe with Hegel in a metaphysical or divine reason inherent in reality and in the process of history. We can no longer believe that all the highest impulses in human nature derive from reason. Least of all can we believe that the appeal to reason will always be the decisive force that determines political and social action. We have learned to penetrate deeply enough into the springs of human action to recognize that what appear on its surface as rational motives are often only rationalizations of our irrational impulses. But none of these disillusionments and discoveries enable us to dispense with reason as the organizing factor in our life and in our society. Just as the approach to a more objective history becomes possible only when we recognize and accept the subjective element which it inevitably contains, so the recognition and acceptance of the irrational element in human behaviour is the first step towards the fuller and more effective development of reason. The fatal barrier to the solution of any problem is to ignore or deny its existence. The gravest obstacle today to the building up of an effective mass democracy comes not from those who are aware of the irrational character of many of our contemporary democratic processes, but from those who are blind to it.

To unmask the irrational by stripping from it its hypocritical fig-leaf of false reason is a salutary and necessary task. But this does not entail a panic flight from reason into the anti-rationalism of Kierkegaard and Dostoevsky or into the irrationalism of Nietzsche ; on the contrary, it is an essential part of the movement towards understanding and overcoming the irrational. Reason is an imperfect instrument : it is good to recognize and study its imperfections. But we should do ill to throw overboard the compass of reason if we hope to advance towards democracy in our time. I cannot indeed share the radiant faith professed by the Utilitarians a century ago and by Mr. Bertrand Russell today in the capacity of reason to transform human nature in a single generation through the processes of education. Reason, like other good things, is sometimes discredited by the exaggerated claims of too enthusiastic pundits. But in that interplay — or, if you like, that struggle — between the forces of good and evil which makes up human nature, reason is, on the whole, to be found on the side of the angels ; and I do not believe that we shall do ourselves anything but harm if we dethrone reason because reason has turned out to be less powerful or less self-sufficient than we thought, and take refuge in a cult of the irrational, even if it disguises itself as the super-rational.

But the concept towards which the modern historian needs most of all to define his attitude is freedom. It is perhaps difficult today to realize the immense impact of the French revolution in the contemporary world. Let us recall the remark of Goethe, that most sober and balanced of men of genius, at Valmy : " Here and now begins a new epoch of world history, and you can say that you were there ". Under the same inspiration Hegel described history as " nothing else than the progress of the consciousness of freedom ". And a hundred years after the great event the cautious Acton was to write : " Never till then had men sought liberty knowing what they sought ". There may be some hyperbole about this claim. But, though some anticipations can be found in primitive Christianity and some perhaps in the English Puritan revolution, it is on the whole fair to attribute to the French revolution the conception of universal liberty as the goal of human endeavour. Hitherto freedom had meant freedom for some people to do certain things. Henceforth the demand was freedom in general, freedom as a matter of principle, freedom for all. The makers of the French revolution did not know what this meant ; indeed, we have been trying to find out ever since.

It is now apparent that the consequence of the French revolution was to change the conception of freedom in two ways. By universalizing freedom, it linked it with equality ; if all were to be free, then all must be equal. Secondly, it gave freedom a material content ; for, once freedom was extended from the limited class which could take economic well-being for granted to the common man who was concerned first and foremost with his daily bread, freedom from the economic constraint of want was clearly just as important as freedom from the political constraint of kings and tyrants. The generation following the French revolution resisted both these conclusions. The third estate, but not the fourth, was the beneficiary of the liberty and equality conferred by the revolution. The new liberal doctrine which denied the competence of the state to intervene in the economic process created a new view of economic liberty and stultified the proposed extension of equality from politics to economics. But after the middle of the nineteenth century this attempt to limit the implications of the revolution broke down under the weight of the new industrial age and of the new mass civilization. In the twentieth century hardly anyone openly contests any longer the two propositions that freedom means freedom for all and therefore equality, and that freedom, if it means anything at all, must include freedom from want.

Pious acceptance of these propositions does not, however, always carry with it willingness to accept their application in terms of policy ; and it is here perhaps that we have to take a stand and define our values. If anyone maintains that it is desirable to achieve the greater freedom of the few at the cost of the lesser freedom of the many, or, in Mandeville's phrase, to make society happy by keeping many people wretched and poor, I can make one of two replies. In the first place, I can assert my view against his as an ultimate difference in values about which one does not argue : one believes in the freedom of the few as a proper aim and purpose or one does not. Secondly, I can reply that the course of history is, according to my interpretation, set against the realization of such a conception of freedom : I might say to the champion of freedom for the few, as I said in my first lecture to the hypothetical champion of monarchy in the United States, that the whole history of the last 150 years is ranged against him. But if he countered me with the charge that I had arrived at my interpretation of history through the medium of my own values, I should have no completely conclusive answer. Perhaps I might say that my interpretation of history seems to me more objective than his, precisely because my values are truer, and therefore lead to less distortion, than his. But this might imply that those values which are approved and realized by the course of history are truer than those which are rejected; and this in turn might involve me in acceptance of a belief in progress in history — a point to which I shall return later.

Having made clear my belief that freedom in our day as a goal of political action and political endeavour must mean freedom for all, let me come to its practical applications and embarrassments. Mill's famous formula recognized liberty for all and therefore comprised equality in liberty. But Mill's liberty was limited to the political and intellectual sphere; when he wrote his famous treatise at the end of the 1850's he had not advanced, even as far as he advanced later, towards the problems of mass civilization and of economic liberty and equality. Even in the political sphere the proposition that my freedom is valid only in so far as it does not limit the freedom of others constitutes a far more serious qualification of absolute liberty than Mill himself realized. But, when we advance beyond the political sphere, the qualification becomes so far-reaching as to necessitate something almost like a re-definition of our whole conception of freedom; and it is at this point that some of those who appeared to accept the doctrine of freedom for all seem to fall by the wayside and revert to the doctrine of freedom for some. For, when we consider the paraphernalia of controls and rationing and taxation necessary to the organization of freedom from want for all, and the restrictions which these involve on the cherished liberties of some, it is not unnatural that some of these some feel that the new freedoms are not an extension of the old freedoms, but their negation. Enough volumes have been written on this theme in the last few years to fill a book-case. You can hardly pick up a newspaper today without finding an article or a letter that re-hashes the familiar argument. Nor can we escape from the dilemma. The price of liberty is the restriction of liberty. The price of some liberty for all is restriction of the greater liberty of some.

While I shall not minimize the reality of this issue and the differences of values involved, more nonsense is talked on the subject of controls than on any other in current politics ; and some of this nonsense we can dispose of forthwith. When I was a boy, one could travel up Whitehall in a horse-bus or a hansom cab or on a bicycle, and, having reached the north end, turn right without more ado into the Strand — a distance of 100 yards or so — to catch one's train at Charing Cross. Today one travels up Whitehall by motor-bus or car, and, having reached the north end and stopped at the traffic lights, one makes a compulsory circuit of Trafalgar Square, stops at more traffic lights, and at last, having travelled well over a quarter of a mile, doubles back into Charing Cross Station in time to miss one's train. What a monstrous infringement of the liberty of the individual ! Could one demand a clearer proof how far we have travelled on the road to serfdom ? Yes, it was better when one could reach Charing Cross in two minutes by travelling 100 yards. Yes, it was better when one could walk into any grocer's shop and buy 5 lb. of sugar for a shilling. The difference is that traffic controls never became an issue of party politics and are now forty years old, so that they have acquired a patina of uncontroversial antiquity which makes it almost sacrilegious to question them ; there is no black market in dodging the traffic lights. The rules are simply accepted, for all their inconvenience to the individual, as a normal, decent amenity of civilized society in a city where the pressure of traffic outruns the comfortable capacity of the streets. When demand outruns supply, and your sense of fairness requires you to make an attempt to satisfy all demands in more or less equal proportions, then there is nothing for it but the queue — the queue at the grocer's shop or the queue at the traffic lights. These are the conditions of scarcity : they will be overcome when we can afford to build enough parkways or fly-overs to carry our traffic and to put enough of the basic necessaries in the shops.

For the present, however, in the crowded mass civilization in which we live, these conditions have become inescapable. To raise the banner of freedom for all is to accept as a normal, decent amenity of the new society those controls which are necessary to effect the orderly equal distribution of scarce resources — whether the resources in question are food and clothing or space on the roads. This does not imply that all existing controls are either well conceived or well administered ; it cannot be assumed without question that even our traffic regulations are the best in the world. But, in principle, scarcity always makes controls necessary. In conditions of scarcity, control to assure equal distribution is not a negation of freedom, but a vital step on the road to freedom — that freedom which can only come in full with full abundance. These problems of distribution are not, in my view, the major problems of freedom in the new society. The economic condition of freedom is the creation of abundance through the right allocation of our human and material resources to the requirements of production ; and here too there will have to be traffic regulations and traffic lights which are restrictions on liberty but are none the less, rightly regarded, necessary milestones on the road to freedom. The political condition of freedom — and economic and political conditions are not really separable — is the realization by the new mass democracy of the principle of government of all and by all and for all. These are high ideals, and politics is the art of the possible. Whole books are written nowadays — though perhaps some of them were hardly necessary — to explain how foolish, and even how wicked, it is to hope to achieve the millennium on earth. It has become fashionable among some writers to dwell with almost sadistic pleasure on the fact of original sin. This is the truth, but certainly not the whole truth, and perhaps not even the most important and relevant part of the truth. Let us at any rate sometimes remind ourselves that mankind is also capable of great achievements and has great achievements to its credit. We may be utopian if we expect to attain our goal. But we shall indubitably fail if we have no goal ahead by which to set our course, or if we shrink from the difficulties and hardships that are encountered on the way.

The French revolution was, in spite of its national origin and title, a European event in an age when Europe still dominated the world. The revolution of today is still more certainly a world event, and its future does not turn on the destiny of a single country. In these lectures I have tried, looking both forward and backward, to chart the course of the revolution in the midst of which we are living. We see its workings everywhere today, sometimes in sharp and rugged outline, sometimes dimly and half hidden beneath an apparently unruffled surface, in Europe, in Asia (perhaps at this moment most of all in Asia), in Africa, in the Americas. We cannot escape it : we can only seek to understand it and to meet it. But I am, for natural reasons, more particularly concerned with the destinies of Great Britain and western Europe and with the implications of the world revolution for these countries. And here one is bound to note discouraging symptoms. Two world wars, of which the first had its main centre, and the second one of its main centres, in western Europe, have helped to create there a condition of material exhaustion and moral lassitude. Material difficulties in the present and graver apprehensions for the future have revealed themselves in those theories of historical decline, of judgment in history, or of a retreat into an ivory tower of pure knowledge, which are so widely current in Great Britain and western Europe at the present time.

Two factors are at work here. The first is the same which accounted for the immense vogue of Spengler's *Decline of the West* in Germany after the first world war. The sense that Germany had lost her place among the great nations began to spread in the interval between the two world wars to the nations of western Europe, and after the second world war struck firm roots there. The shifting of the centre of gravity of the world to other continents translated itself into a belief in universal decay. In Great Britain, in particular, the temptation to identify the end of British supremacy with the impending end of civilization became increasingly hard to resist. The almost unchallenged British supremacy of the nineteenth century was the result of a fortunate opportunity seized with energy and enterprise — the long start enjoyed by Britain in that complex series of developments known as the Industrial revolution. It was an accident whose results could not last for ever. By the beginning of the twentieth century the British lead was being overtaken by Germany and by the United States. After the first world war the world economy and the world financial system, built as it was on the international division of labour between metropolitan industrial nations and dependent colonial peoples, crumbled in ruins : after the second world war Great Britain — like much of the rest of the world — was the impoverished debtor of the United States. Whatever the situation of the rest of the world had been, and whatever the prospects of civilization in general, these straitened circumstances in Britain, and the sense of economic dependence succeeding economic supremacy, could hardly fail to encourage an inclination to look back to a golden age in the past and promote pessimistic estimates of future potentialities.

The second factor in the spread of a pessimistic outlook was domestic. The vast majority of the ruling groups in Great Britain, in every branch of the national life, still belong, either by birth or by adoption, to the class which was the main beneficiary of British prosperity and power before 1914, and are therefore under the impression of a steep decline not only in British power and prosperity as a whole, but, within the country, in the power and prosperity of the class to which they belong. Before 1914 concessions by the British ruling class to other groups in the interests of social cohesion and social stability had been made out of a rising standard of living. They had been made at the cost of a curtailment of a natural increase, but not — except for a very small and highly privileged group — at the cost of an actual decline. In the last thirty years the situation has changed rapidly ; and, with the decline in Britain's power and prosperity, the cost both of armaments and of social services has been met by progressively depressing the living standards of a large part of the ruling class. There is thus a dual reason for the pessimistic and fatalistic mood which has become visible in the British approach to contemporary problems : the decline in British power and prosperity, and the decline in the power and prosperity of that group in British society which has a paramount share in determining policy and opinion. It is on any reckoning extraordinarily difficult for groups or individuals who have enjoyed prosperity under a certain dispensation, and learned to regard the beliefs on which that dispensation rested as eternally valid, to re-adapt themselves to a world in which that dispensation has passed away for ever and its beliefs are shown to be no more than a reflexion and expression of the interests that upheld it. Once upon a time I had an uncle who beguiled his declining years by explaining to all who would listen that the world was going rapidly from bad to worse. But, being by nature a cheerful soul, he always ended his lament with the same aphorism : " Well, if we *are* all going down the drain, let us go down the drain with our top-hats on ". This country today is full of old gentlemen — some of them not so old, and some of them in important places — who are far less worried by the prospect of going down the drain than by the prospect that the gale may blow off their top-hats. Respect for tradition is all right in its way, provided we do not smother ourselves with it. Nostalgia for the ruins on the shore that lies behind is a natural and venial human sentiment. But indulgence in it may easily become politically fatal.

It is tempting to discover here what I will not call a law of history, but the explanation of a common historical phenomenon. Those powerful and decisive historical upheavals which we call revolutions, without confining the term to upheavals which are brought about or accompanied by violence, have frequently led to a displacement of power and leadership from one country to another, as if it was not possible for the same rôle to be played by the same country in successive and different periods of history ; and, if this is true, I would suspect that the explanation lies in the difficulty which occurs in inducing any powerfully established ruling group to abandon the privileges which it enjoyed in the period of its supremacy and to adapt itself to the revolutionary process of transition from one period to the next. No inherent reason exists why we in this country should succumb to the same experience. It does indeed seem to me impossible for external reasons that Great Britain should regain the position of world-wide supremacy which she exercised in the nineteenth century. But, if existing ruling groups can be adapted to the revolutionary changes through which we are passing, or be replaced by other groups, no necessary obstacle stands in the way of further progress towards the new society whose outlines have already begun to shape themselves. This, however, involves the obligation to accept and complete the revolution on which we have willy-nilly embarked. It is only in recent years that the notion of radical innovation has brought pallor to our cheeks. " Nothing less than a convulsion that will shake the globe to its centre ", wrote Burke, a sound conservative, " can ever restore the European nations to that liberty by which they were once so much distinguished." And Acton, who was also no radical, spoke of revolution as " the method of modern progress " whose function it was " to shake off the past " and " rescue the world from the reign of the dead ". It was perhaps a better Britain in which even the Right were on nodding terms with revolution than the Britain of today in which even the Left will be found, when the moment comes for the autopsy, to have died with " Safety first " graven on their hearts. Three broad possibilities confront this country at the present time : sudden disaster, slow stagnation and decay such as once overtook the civilizations of Byzantium and of Spain, and re-adaptation to the needs and conditions of a new historical period. The one thing we cannot do is to return to the shore whence we have come. Disaster might overwhelm us through events largely beyond our control. But the possibility of a tornado does not excuse negligent or faulty seamanship. We still have a good chance of coming through if we boldly face the prospect ahead.

And this brings me back to the point from which I started : whether we are to think of the century and a half since the French revolution — together with the other great events which changed the face of the world in the closing years of the eighteenth century — as a period of advance or decline. If I sometimes in these lectures or elsewhere said hard things about the nineteenth-century order, I should like here to make full amends. We still stand, perhaps, rather too near to the Victorian age : we can see too clearly the warts on its face. But I have no doubt that it will in future, and in virtue primarily of the British achievement, rank as one of the great ages of history. Nor do I believe that the nineteenth-century achievement represents a self-stultifying climax, a dead end in which humanity has come to a full stop. I believe that the future will take these foundations and build fresh achievements on them, though I should refuse altogether to guess whether this will happen at once or after a more or less prolonged interval or interruption, and whether those peoples who participated most actively in the great nineteenth-century achievements will be among the leaders in the next advance. But even if I were compelled to despair of the ability of the country to which I belong, or of the group to which I belong, to share in a further advance, even if I were compelled to regard them as no more than stately relics left behind on the backward shore, this would still not provide me with sufficient evidence to support the unlikely conclusion that the process of history has come to an end. The race will not stop simply because some of the runners fall out.

It will be perceived that I am in some sense committing myself to the old-fashioned, discarded, discredited belief in progress in history. But let me be clear in what sense. I believe in progress in neither of the senses current in the nineteenth century. I do not believe in laws of history comparable to the laws of science in accordance with which human affairs continually advance through certain regular processes towards some higher condition (and equally little in laws in accordance with which they successively or alternately advance and decline). Nor do I believe in the working of providence through the processes of history to reward human merit or to punish human sin. Nor do I profess to offer any objective definition of progress. Progress is just what it says, a moving on — a conscious moving on towards purposes which are felt to be worthy of human faith and human endeavour. These purposes and the actions which they inspire, like all human purposes and actions, are blended of good and evil in varying proportions. The purposes and actions of one group or of one generation are sifted and tested, accepted and rejected, by its contemporaries or its successors; yet progress is clearly meaningless unless one believes (whether or not the belief is supported by some religions or secular faith) that the good in mankind sufficiently balances the evil not merely to keep the ship afloat and provide for its navigation, but to inspire some sense of goal or destination. Certainly, without the hypothesis of progress, there is no history. Men emerge into history when they become aware of themselves as having a past, and consciously use the achievements of the past as a starting point for future achievement. The unhistorical peoples are those who have no aspirations, those who do not look backwards because they do not look forwards. Faith in the future is a condition of meaningful interest in the past.

If, however, I were asked to define the content of progress, I should fall back on the well-worn word " freedom " ; and, if I were asked to define the goal towards which we shall seek to move at the present time, I should say " freedom for all ", or " freedom for many ", in contrast with the " freedom for some " which has been the great achievement of the recent past. And, if I were asked to define freedom, I do not think I could do better than the definition of Berdyaev (which is indeed not altogether new) : " The opportunity for creative activity ". This definition includes within itself the old and unsatisfyingly negative definition of freedom as " the recognition of necessity " ; for creative activity implies an understanding of the conditions in which such activity can be pursued. The world of politics — and what is not political today ? — is the world of history. No valuable political activity can be carried on without that knowledge of conditions and possibilities which history affords. No history, no freedom : and, conversely, no freedom, no history. In these lectures I have tried to show the process of interaction between past and future, between objective and subjective, between the determined and the free, which I believe to be the essential element of history and the essential element of freedom, and to show how it is possible to derive from it not the absolute and irrevocable judgments which we expect from the scientist, but the critical insights which belong to the study of history and politics. And these critical insights, which constantly seek to revise the insights of others, are themselves subject to constant criticism and revision. The one absolute in history is change. Nobody can doubt today that we live in a world which is constantly being transformed before our eyes. Let me refer again to the words of Tocqueville which I took in my first lecture as the motto of this series and to which I have more than once returned in the course of it : " A new science of politics is indispensable to a new world ". It would be a pity if we in this country failed to play our part in working out, in theory and in practice, this new science because " we obstinately fix our eyes on the ruins which may still be descried upon the shore we have left, while the current sweeps us . . . backward towards the gulf ".

THE END

PRINTED BY R. & R. CLARK, LTD., EDINBURGH